KINDLINGS

Other books by Vic Jackopson

1978 Evangelism Explosion (U.K. Edition) - edited
1980 Evangelism Explosion Handbook
1980 Prison to Pulpit (Marshall Pickering)
1981 Hitch-Hiker's Guide to Heaven
1990 Prison to Pulpit (2nd Edition)
1994 Good, Morning Disciple

Booklets:
1980 Just Grace
1989 Hope Now
1989 Grow Now
1990 Recycled

KINDLINGS

50 Daily
FireStarter
Bible Studies
from
ROMANS 8

Vic Jackopson

Illustrated by Ian Smith

ADVIDUS
COMMUNICATIONS

Biblical References, unless otherwise stated, are
from the New International Version

Copyright © 1994 by Vic Jackopson
All Illustrations Copyright 1994 Ian Smith/Advidus

The right of Vic Jackopson to be identified as the author of
the Work has been asserted by him in accordance with the
Copyright, Designs and Patents Act 1988

This Edition Published 1994 by
Advidus Communications

1 3 5 7 9 10 8 6 4 2

All rights reserved. No storing, retrieving, reproducing or transmitting of any part
of this publication without prior written permission of the publisher. Not to be
circulated in any form or binding or cover other than that in which it is published
and without a similar condition imposed on the subsequent purchaser

ISBN 1-899027-00-9

Typeset by Advidus Communications
Printed and bound in Great Britain by Cox & Wyman Ltd,
Reading, Berkshire

Advidus Communications
PO Box 544, Southgate,
London N14 7EZ

CONTENTS

Acknowledgments 6
Dedication 7
Preface 8
Daily Studies 9
Prayer of Faith 109
Hymn 110
Bibliography 111

ACKNOWLEDGMENTS

This book would not have been possible without the hard work, time and patience of my wife, Sue and the generous cooperation of Rev. Bob Archer of Spurgeon's College, Rev. Frank Fitzsimmonds and Mrs. Sylvie Pierce who have read the manuscript and made many helpful suggestions.

Quotes of George MacDonald from *Discovering the Character of God*, edited by Michael R. Phillips, Bethany House Publishers, Minneapolis, Minnesota.

DEDICATION

In Memory of the late Sir Cyril Black, friend and mentor, without whose help Hope Now Ministries may still have been a dream.

PREFACE

Two thirds of the way through this chapter eight of Romans Paul gives the encouraging word that "The Spirit helps us in our weakness."(v.23). At that point in my writing I felt as a mountaineer must sometimes feel. High enough to look back at marvellous vistas but now close enough to see the most difficult and arduous part of the climb ahead.

This is one of the great, if not the greatest Everest Chapters of Scripture. There have been times when I have literally burst out - Wow! that's great and with racing pulse tried to capture on the page the laughter, the ecstasy, the sheer wonder of new discovery. At other times, vulnerability and frustration have driven me back to my knees to look up again as an inquisitive child to the face of Abba, Father, and pester Him with more questions than a three year old.

He does not disappoint. Neither will you be disappointed if you take a few minutes each day to read these devotions, and meditate on the suggested further reading in the Scripture. You will not agree with everything I say any more than I agree with everything George McDonald has written. But I have, in reading his *Discovering the Character of God* been so delighted with his insights that I have given you a snippet each day - relevant to the theme.

When you come to something which makes you stroke your chin, persevere. Most of God's truths are not left scattered on the surface but lie a little deeper than prying and mischievous eyes can see. Take time to dig beneath the obvious. There are treasures to be found.

Vic Jackopson

Southampton
February 1994

Therefore, there is now no condemnation for those who are in Christ Jesus (Romans 8:1)

DAY 1

Unrelentingly, the wind ripped across the flat Somerset countryside, penetrating all but the warmest anoraks or blankets worn by the summer solstice devotees mustered on Glastonbury's exposed Tor. The still gloomy western sky at their backs, they huddled in dreary expectation awaiting the sunrise.

Why had two or three hundred people left the snug comfort of their duvets for such an inhospitable vantage point? Quaint English eccentricity? An excuse for an all night party of hash and a swig of lager?

For some, undoubtedly, the exercise held deep religious, even pagan, significance. Advocates of the New Age movement probably saw mysterious symbolism for the dawning of the Age of Aquarius.

As I mused over the possibilities, the first hint of gold peeked over the far horizon, and I remembered another dawn. A dawn which heralded the authentic New Age. A dawn which would compel the apostle Paul to see in it a new beginning, a new era. A dawn which would dispel the darkness of an old order which had lasted from Eden to Good Friday, from Adam to Jesus.

In speaking of the eternal consequences of that new day, Paul would always talk of Now.

> NOW righteousness would no longer come from the imposition of law, but through faith in Christ for all who believe (Romans 3.21-22)
> NOW, justified by Christ's blood (5.9)
> NOW, reconciled to God by Christ's death (5.10)
> NOW, saved because Christ lived sinlessly (5.10)
> NOW, slaves of righteousness and freed from sin's authority (6.19)
> NOW, willing servants of the Spirit instead of reluctant observers of law (7.6)
> NOW, for those in Christ, no more condemnation (8.1)

KINDLING QUOTE

"No man is condemned for anything he has done; .... He is condemned for not coming out of darkness, for not coming to the light, the Living God, who sent the Light, His son, into the world to guide him home."

- all quotes from George MacDonald in *Discovering the Character of God*

DAY 1

The judgement on sin was unchanged because God would not violate his own standard of justice. The penalty of death which He imposed from the courts of heaven, unrepealed, led Jesus as a willing sacrifice to the cross so that the punishment would not fall on us. Those who, by faith, died with Christ were also raised with Christ to live in Christ, and for such there is now no condemnation. Such will live with full confidence in Him.

Perhaps then you will understand why on that cold Glastonbury hill top, as the sun rose, I filled my lungs and shouted in a loud voice the Easter declaration CHRIST IS RISEN. HALLELUJAH. HE IS RISEN INDEED.

As you read Colossians 1.15-23 meditate for a few minutes on verse 22.

FIRESTARTER VERSE

I tell you, now is the time of God's favour, now is the day of salvation (2 Corinthians 6.2b)

Because through Christ Jesus the law of the Spirit of life set me free from the law of sin and death (8.2)

DAY 2

The man who never made a mistake probably made little else, but when a mistake is made, it is profitable in that you may learn from it and try to correct it, though the latter is not always possible.

How many have, like me, looked at Paul's inner conflict in Romans 7 and presumed he was talking about his pre-Christian experience? I have even preached that. But I confess it, it was an honest mistake.

He was, as will be seen by his use of the present tense, talking about his ongoing experience. He longed after holiness, but like all other believers, found that road strewn with one failure after another.

There are two common misunderstandings about Christianity. The first is that by being good a person may earn salvation. No, says the apostle! Whether as a Jew under the law, or a gentile under conscience, there is none good enough to come near to God. (Romans 3.23) Therefore, the only hope for the sinner is Christ. By believing that He paid the just penalty for man's sin on the cross, the person who believes by faith is freely justified by God's grace to receive what Paul calls redemption - that is, freedom from the penalty.

The second misunderstanding is that when somebody becomes a Christian, automatically that person becomes good. Nothing could be further from the truth. That is what Paul has been saying in chapter 7.

Even though new spiritual desires are prompted by the Holy Spirit within, we still live in human bodies which are, by nature, sin loving.

Paul's cry, "Who will rescue me from this body of death?" is not the despair of an unbeliever, rather the frustration of one who longs in his mind to be free from sin, yet finds the struggle all but overwhelming

And indeed it would be, if it were not for Christ and His conquering the consequence of our sin.

KINDLING QUOTE

"The law has been fully prevented from working its full end."

DAY 2

"There is now no condemnation" sets the scene for a chapter in which the weak, failing, struggling believer is given a new understanding of God's grace to uphold and sustain. Hope and confidence are its recurring themes. There is no condemnation, no accusing finger, because that which stood opposed to us, namely, "the law of sin and death", has itself come under a greater condemnation - it has been made impotent. Christ has conquered! This is why, after Paul's cry of frustration (7.24), he immediately explodes with intoxicating gratitude as the reverberations of Good Friday burst in upon his mind. "Thanks be to God," he rejoices, "through our Lord Jesus Christ." (7.25) The grace which brought life through Christ at the start of the Christian life is unchanged and effective in the life of the believer, even though he fall again and again.

This does not mean to say that we should not fight sin in our lives. As we shall see later, one of the proofs of our belonging to Christ is that we join the struggle against sin.

The true believer will always long for holiness and even though he fail many times to live up to his or her calling, the prompting of the Holy Spirit will always be in that direction.

It will be helpful to you now to read the whole of Romans 7. Happy hunting.

FIRESTARTER VERSE

Now the Lord is the Spirit, and where the Spirit of the Lord is, there is freedom. And we, who with unveiled faces all reflect the Lord's glory, are being transformed into his likeness with ever increasing glory, which comes from the Lord, who is Spirit
(2 Corinthians 3.17-18)

For what the law was powerless to do in that it was weakened by the sinful nature, God did by sending his own Son in the likeness of sinful man to be a sin offering (8.3a)

DAY 3

As a diagnostic tool, the X-ray has been used as a standard procedure for revealing the location and extent of such diverse ailments as broken bones and cancer. That is its strength. When it comes to mending bones or removing growths, other tools and procedures are needed.

As a diagnostic means of exposing our human brokenness and dis-ease, the written law of God achieved in the moral sphere what the X-ray has done in the physical. By setting a standard of wholeness and righteousness it showed the sheer extent, the universality, of our sinfulness.

When it came to dealing with sin the law was inadequate for the task. It could list the prohibitions. But it could not effect a change in human nature, any more than setting a speed limit means all motorists will drive within it. The weakness was not in the law but in the sinful, self-indulgent environment of humanity in which it operated. Even those who tried to obey it were seduced by pride (Romans 2.17) and perverted God's intention of life giving laws into the deathly minutiae of nit-picking self-glorifying rules and regulations. "... you hypocrites!", said Jesus. "You give a tenth of your spices - mint, dill and cummin. But you have neglected the more important matters of the law - justice, mercy and faithfulness. .... You blind guides! You strain out a gnat but swallow a camel." (Matthew 23.23,24)

The remedy for sin did not lie in the law any more than the cure for cancer lies in repeated exposure to more and more X-ray. Once the law had done its job, the time was right for God to act. "But when the time had fully come, God sent his Son, born of a woman, born under law, to redeem those under law...." (Galatians 4.4,5)

KINDLING QUOTE

"If Jesus suffered for men, it was because His Father suffers for men."

13

DAY 3

The contrast between the heavenly and earthly status could not be greater. Literally the Greek reads "The Son of Himself". John calls Him, "the only begotten of God, who was in the bosom of the Father." (John 1.18 AV)

This one was sent in the likeness of sinful man, or more literally, flesh of sin. He who was in His very nature God (Philippians 2.6) became like us, in a body capable of sinning and yet unlike us in that His will never gave in to selfish cravings.

It is important to note that Paul does not say "in the likeness of flesh". That would lead to the docetic heresy that Jesus was not real flesh and blood - that He was a mere phantom. John calls such an idea "the spirit of the antichrist", because without a real body subject to human temptation, His perfection would be a phoney innocence. He is an offering for sin only because He is the true representative of man, tempted as we are and yet without sin.

What the law could not achieve because it was over and above human flesh, Jesus accomplished by becoming human flesh. By coming in human flesh, He exploded the gnostic myth that the flesh is, in itself, evil.

As you read John 1.1-18 meditate on verse 12. If you have never received Him, read the prayer on page 109.... You may like to make it your prayer today.

FIRESTARTER VERSE

**If you belong to Christ, then you are Abraham's seed, and heirs according to promise
(Galatians 3.29)**

To be a sin offering. And so he condemned sin in sinful man (8.3b)

DAY 4

During any war there are many deeds of shameful depravity which are occasionally relieved by courageous acts of heroic humanity. The United States were torn apart by a savage Civil War which set brother against brother. That conflict generated stories, which in some cases have developed a life of their own in the retelling, but I have no reason to suppose that this one is anything but a straightforward account of what happened.

A band of Confederate soldiers had been caught, but in the confusion of battle, one man had managed to escape. The next day the prisoners were lined up in front of a firing squad. Suddenly, a young man ran into the camp, identifying himself as the escapee. He pleaded with the Union Captain to let him take the place of one of the older family men, because he was himself single. The Captain agreed and moments later the young man lay dead alongside his companions. One man walked out of the camp a free man, but not before he had erected a simple memorial engraved with the man's name and an inscription, "He died in my place."

I guess that father never forgot the lad who died for him. Neither can the Christian ever forget that Jesus came as an offering for sin to save those who are condemned because of sin.

Literally the Greek reads "for sin" but the N.I.V. is probably correct in this instance to translate it "to be an offering for sin". *Peri hamartia* was used when translating the term "sin offering" from the Hebrew text of the Old Testament to the Greek of the New Testament. For example, when Hebrews 10:6 was translated directly from Psalm 40:6 the "sin offerings" are called *peri hamartias*. It makes sense, therefore, to use it in this technical way.

Biblically, the concept of Jesus as an offering for sin is unquestionable. Why, even in this very letter, Paul explains justification as a sacrifice which would turn away God's wrath by satisfying His justice. (Romans 3.25) All who have faith in His blood would be able to say, like the soldier at His saviour's grave, "He died in my place."

KINDLING QUOTE

"It is God who has sacrificed His own Son for us. There was no other way of getting the gift of Himself into our hearts."

DAY 4

*Bearing shame and scoffing rude
In my place condemned He stood
Sealed my pardon with His blood
Hallelujah, what a Saviour.*

It is important in any battle to recognise who the enemy really is. The unbeliever hears about the wrath of God and presumes that God is hostile toward him. God is not. He is hostile toward sin and it is sin, the great enemy of man, which is under attack.

For this battle Jesus came. In conquering the law of sin and death, He turned the tables. That which condemned us has itself been condemned. Its residual power is doomed. It no longer has any authority over the believer's ultimate destiny.

Read about your deliverance in Romans 5.

FIRESTARTER VERSE

God made him who had no sin to become sin for us, so that in him we might become the righteousness of God
(2 Corinthians 5.21)

In order that the righteous requirements of the law might be fully met in us, who do not live according to the sinful nature but according to the Spirit (8.4)

DAY 5

Augustine's dictum that, "Law was given that grace might be sought; grace was given that the law might be fulfilled," true as it is, needs one word-change to suit this text. Law was given that grace might be sought, Christ was given that the law might be fulfilled.

Paul's pen must have hovered over the page as he wrote "in order that ..." There was so much that he could have written after those words as the purpose for which Christ came into the world:

In order that our sins might be forgiven (Matthew 26.28)
In order that our consciences might be cleansed (Hebrews 9.14)
In order that we might be justified (Romans 5.9)
In order that we might be redeemed (1 Peter 1.18)
In order that we might be purified (1 John 1.7)
In order that we might be reconciled to God (Colossians 1.20)
In order that we might be presented to God on the day of Judgement, holy, without blemish and free from accusation (Colossians 1.22)
In order that Christ might atone for our sins (1 John 4.10)
In order that we might know God's love (Romans 5.8)

Yes, these and more, are all part of the treasure of hope stored up for us in heaven; the unsearchable riches of Christ. But these are not what Paul had in mind. It is the vindication of God Himself. He whose righteous decrees are part of His very justice will save us from our sins, but not at the expense of His own nature. The law may be weakened, but not God, nor His lasting claim upon us to live in accordance with His ways.

KINDLING QUOTE

"We can be sons and daughters saved into the bliss of our being, only by choosing God for the Father he is, and doing his will - yielding ourselves true sons and daughters to the absolute Father."

DAY 5

A person may declare that he will break the law of gravity as he throws himself off a tower block, but when he meets the pavement below it is not gravity that has been broken. However, the physical law of gravity may be suspended for a while by another law - the law of aero-dynamics. Eventually, though, what goes up within the gravitational pull of the earth must come down. The bird or the plane must eventually land, and thereby prove the law of gravity.

The same is true of God's moral law. It may appear that it is weakened by the law of sin at work in human hearts. It may even be forgotten, in the same way that a bird with wings to fly pays scant attention to the law of gravity. But God will be vindicated either in the judgement of sinners, or in the more positive effect of Christ's life and death in the believer.

Notice how the location of this fulfilment of the law is in us: we who live according to the Spirit, who have God's law written, no longer on tablets of stone, but upon our hearts. There is a mystery in this interchange whereby He who knew no sin, became sin, in order that we might become the very righteousness of God, (see 2 Corinthians 5.21). But in the implications there is no mystery. We who have been freed from the kingdom of sin are called to be holy. As Jesus put it, "For them I sanctify myself, that they too may be truly sanctified." (John 17.19)

As you read Galatians 5.13-26 ask God to reproduce within you the fruit of the Spirit today (see v. 22).

FIRESTARTER VERSE

**For all of you who were baptised into Christ have clothed yourselves with Christ
(Galatians 3.27)**

Those who live according to the sinful nature have their minds set on what that nature desires; but those who live in accordance with the Spirit have their minds set on what the Spirit desires (8.5)

DAY 6

Brothers born to the same parents, living in the same environment, are rarely ever alike when it comes to personal interests. Even as babies and toddlers they show a natural inclination to do the things they want to do. One may like the outdoors and physical pursuits more than his timid brother. The other may be happier talking up a storm or tinkering with model railways. As they develop, the differences may become even more marked. Muscles, riding and scrimmage for the stronger while his brother prefers Mahler, reading and Scrabble. The natural bent determines the aspirations; so it is a wise parent who recognises their individual personalities and encourages each to become the best they can be in their own field.

Personality, however, is not the determining factor when it comes to the choice of which kingdom we live in. All are born under the curse of sin and have a sinful nature. "There is no difference, for all have sinned and fall short of the glory of God." (Romans 3.22-23) How then can Paul talk about some living according to sin while others live by the Spirit?

The answer lies somewhere between the statement of fact in our text and backward in time to a choice or choices. Those who live according to the sinful nature have developed a pattern of behaviour through a multitude of self-indulgent choices. In each decision, there has been the option to choose generosity over greed, love instead of lust, humility in preference to pride and others before self. It is not that the sinful mind never makes the right choice, but that the established pattern of the will is alien to God and self-indulgent. That becomes the mind-set.

What distinguishes those living according to the Spirit from their unbelieving past life-style is not necessarily a dramatic change. Though fighting against sin is a real demand and must be taken seriously, none of us, not even the most saintly, are ever completely free from its moral snares. What makes the difference is that somewhere along the way, presented with the Good News about new life in Christ, we have exchanged our natural state of sinfulness for a God-given righteousness. As Paul says elsewhere, "This righteousness from God comes through faith in Jesus Christ to all who believe." (Romans 3.22)

KINDLING QUOTE

"Obedience is the joining of the links of the eternal round. Obedience is but the other side of the creative will. Will is God's will; obedience is man's will; the two make one."

DAY 6

This does not mean that the believer never sins. Indeed, he may be no better than those of no faith. But if the Holy Spirit has taken up residence, He brings conviction of sin and selfishness. He challenges the old mind-set every time the Christian comes to the Father in prayer. If a person is truly in Christ, a desire to please Him and not to grieve the Spirit will bring changes in behaviour. (Ephesians 4.30) Very soon the mind-set is no longer on sin but on the Spirit and His leading. Now the struggle of which Paul spoke so graphically (7.14-25) is no longer theory, but daily warfare to prove who is Lord.

Read what Jesus had to say about the hazards of having two masters in Matthew 6.19-34.

Even as babies and toddlers they show a natural inclination to do the things they want to do.

FIRESTARTER VERSE

... live by the Spirit, and you will not gratify the desires of the sinful nature (Galatians 5.16)

The mind of the sinful man is death, but the mind controlled by the Spirit is life (8.6)

DAY 7

In the period of Mengistu's presidency over Ethiopia, many Christians suffered persecution under the ruling Communists. Alemu Serenesa, one of their own evangelists, served no less than seven terms of imprisonment for preaching about faith in Christ.

"Either deny Christ or be shot", threatened one of his guards during his second imprisonment.

To recant on his faith was for Alemu unthinkable, but like any loving son, he was concerned about the grief this would cause to his mother. When she came the next day to deliver the daily ration of food, he told her, as gently as he knew how, about the ultimatum and the possibility of death in the morning.

Her response startled and delighted him. "Son," she said, "If you deny Christ, don't ever come home."

"Praise the Lord," he answered. "It's good to have such a mother."

That night Alemu's tormentor and would-be executioner died. The cause of death remained a mystery.

The truth is that the guard was dead before he died. His life, his mentality, his behaviour were all death. His mind-set was on the sinful nature and so long as he gave into its sadistic passion or indeed, any other ungodly desire, he was himself living under the penalty of death. (Romans 3.23) At any time before that fateful night, he could and indeed should have owned up to the sin in his life, repented of it and turned to Christ for forgiveness, exchanging his living death for a new and godly life. I have no doubt that my fellow evangelist would have preferred this to his death: but without repentance, the mind-set of the sinful man is death.

In contrast, the mind-set which willingly submits to the Holy Spirit, because of Christ's sacrifice for sin, is destined for eternal life. The life lived in the present is merely a foretaste, a deposit on an inevitable inheritance of everlasting life. If Alemu had been shot, he would not have been shot to death, except in the physical realm. He would have been shot into life - eternal life.

KINDLING QUOTE

"The only vengeance worth having on sin is to make the sinner himself the executioner."

DAY 7

What is at stake here is not merely a matter of profession. A person may seemingly accept the forgiveness and grace of God but still hold on to sin and reject the controlling influence of the Holy Spirit. Is such a one any better than the openly rebellious? No! Surely worse! Death is still at work unless there is a true repentance and loathing of all that is alien to God. Life comes only when a person receives the Holy Spirit. He is not a genie in a lamp, to be at our beck and call as though we were His master. Quite the contrary. He wants total control so that He may bring us fully into the life which God has prepared for all whom He loves.

As you read John 6.47-71 ask God to show you the special significance of verse 63 for today's walk.

FIRESTARTER VERSE

To those who by persistence in doing good seek glory, honour and immortality, he will give eternal life
(Romans 2.7)

And peace (8.6)

DAY 8

Little do most people realise that when they moan, "There is no peace ... for the wicked", they are echoing one of Isaiah's prophecies which finds its fulfilment in this and other New Testament texts. (Isaiah 57.21)

The peace spoken of here is not merely the absence of conflict. One may find a measure of tranquillity in the avoidance of conflict. I once knew a woman who became furious with her husband because whenever she became contentious he, without saying a word, simply left the house to go for a quiet walk.

Neither is it the peace of forgetfulness which buries the sins of the past, by the activities of the present, neglectful of what a famous American preacher used to call "payday some day", in the future.

Nor yet is it the peace borne out of the arrogance of Pharisaism which presumes to have arrived already at the right side of God's bargaining counter due to religious observance. (Luke 18.11,12)

KINDLING QUOTE

"No man is ever condemned for any sin except one - that he will not leave his sins, come out of them, and be a child of Him who is his father."

whenever she became contentious...

DAY 8

It is a peace the world cannot give. A peace only available through the One who said, "... my peace I give you." (John 14.27) It is peace with God which produces in us the fruits of righteousness, and leads to "the peace of God, which transcends all understanding" (Philippians 4.7). It is none other than the *shalom* of the Old Testament covenant which Moses passed on to Aaron as God's blessing to Israel.

> *"The Lord bless you and keep you;*
> *the Lord make his face shine upon you*
> *and be gracious to you;*
> *the Lord turn his face toward you and give you peace."*
> *(Numbers 6.24-26)*

After the chaos of Israel's constant rebellion against her God and His holy laws (Isaiah 57.17), God renewed His covenant of peace, not because of their obedience, but due to His unfailing love and compassion (Isaiah 54.10). He would send one of whom eventually the world would sing, "For to us a child is born, to us a son is given ... he will be called Wonderful, Counsellor, Mighty God, Everlasting Father, Prince of Peace". (Isaiah 9.6 AV)

Peace with God is not something we achieve, as though by a determined surge of goodness, we could reset the scales of justice which have found us wanting. "We have," says the apostle, "been justified through faith, we have peace with God through our Lord Jesus Christ, through whom we have gained access by faith into this grace in which we now stand." (Romans 5.1-2) Ours was the sin which created the hostility and made us enemies of God, but His was the grace whereby we were reconciled to him through the death of His Son" (5.10).

However, the life controlled by the Spirit is not only at peace with God, but has also the peace of God. It is the fruit given by the Holy Spirit to all who submit to His control. One of the surest signs that the Spirit is winning that control is a deepening sense of peace and freedom from anxiety.

Look at Philippians 4.1-9 to see how to deal with anxiety and gain God's peace.

FIRESTARTER VERSE

Righteousness and peace kiss each other
(Psalm 85.10b)

The sinful mind is hostile to God. It does not submit to God's law, nor can it do so. Those controlled by the sinful nature cannot please God (8.7-8)

DAY 9

Just as the hunter was about to pull the trigger, the bear who was in his sights asked his would-be assassin, "Why do you want to shoot me?"

"Oh," replied the hunter, "I just want your fur coat."

"That's fine," said the bear. "All I want is my lunch. Let's sit down and negotiate a compromise."

They did! The hunter wore his new fur coat just at the point when the bear finished his meal.

Presumably, the moral of this Russian tale is never to compromise with a bear unless you wish to wear one.

To compromise with sin is equally deadly for, just as righteousness leads to peace, so sin induces hostility toward God. Paul reminded the Christians at Colosse of this when he recalled for them, "Once you were alienated from God and were enemies in your minds because of your evil behaviour." (Colossians 1.21)

Note the direction of the hostility. It is not that God is hostile to man. Quite the contrary. It is sinful humanity which directs its hostility toward God. The phenomenon of hostility borne out of guilt is common enough in human behaviour. We see it for example when an adulterer becomes violent towards his innocent and even loving wife.

It is not without significance that the prophets referred to rebellious Israel as an adulterous nation. To choose other than God is to turn away from His ways and His good pleasure. James puts it even more strongly. He says, "You adulterous people, don't you know that friendship with the world is hatred toward God? Anyone who chooses to be a friend of the world becomes an enemy of God." (James 4.4)

God is implacably opposed to sin. Therefore, the mind that is bent on sin can cause Him no pleasure. It is only in living a life worthy of the Lord that we are able to please Him. (Colossians 1.10)

KINDLING QUOTE

"God chooses to be good, otherwise he would not be God: man must choose to be good, otherwise he (she) cannot be the son (daughter) of God." *(Brackets my own)*

DAY 9

The sinful mind, that of the unbeliever, is a mind controlled by selfish desire, unless and until it is delivered by the greater power of Christ, and through Him reconciled to God and thereafter controlled by the Spirit. It really boils down to who is pulling the strings. Pinnochio may have sung for all he was worth about having "no strings to hold me down" but he very soon learned the controlling power of selfishness.

The unbeliever, on the other hand, must day by day, even moment by moment, reject the enticing and controlling power of sin by calling on his higher power - that of the Holy Spirit. He may sometimes fail - indeed he will - but he must never give up that struggle. If he really loves God, his desire will be to fight sin. Rarely ever will overt rebellion trouble the believer but little compromises lead to larger consequences. Watch out for the bear!

As you read the first twelve verses of 1 Thessalonians 4 note how to please God (v.1) and practice it.

FIRESTARTER VERSE

Set your mind on things above, not on earthly things (Colossians 3.2)

You, however, are controlled not by the sinful nature but by the Spirit, if the Spirit of God lives in you (8.9a)

DAY 10

When I was in the former Czechoslovakia, in that part now called Slovakia, I was told that Skoda meant "What a pity". Therefore, I call this a Skoda verse because the N.I.V. translators have needlessly moved from the literal meaning captured more successfully in the A.V. which reads: "But ye are not in the flesh, but in the Spirit, if so be that the Spirit of God dwell in you." Admittedly, the final result is the same. But what a pity to lose the picture of being either "in the flesh" or "in the Spirit".

You can tell a great deal about the people who live in a house by looking at what is there. The decor, the furnishings, the ornaments, pictures and general ambience all give clues to the would-be Sherlock Holmes. A clearer picture may be discovered by looking at the books, newspapers, periodicals and record collection. All of this without even meeting the family. If you lived in that home for a while and noted which T.V. programmes and videos were watched and how each individual related to others in the family, you would be able to give an even clearer definition of what kind of people lived in that particular house.

Likewise we may judge for ourselves by our behaviour which house we live in, the house of "the flesh" or the house of "the Spirit". If one is living at the mercy of instincts and giving in to self-centred impulses as the norm of life, that is the life controlled by the sinful nature, the flesh. It takes on the character of what is brought in, or allowed in, just like any home. Whereas the life in which the Holy Spirit takes up residence will have in it those attributes of the Spirit: love, joy, peace, patience, kindness, goodness, faithfulness, gentleness and self-control.

It is not for us to judge others but we must judge ourselves and ask the questions, "Am I living in the flesh or am I living in the Spirit?" Does the sinful nature have control or does the Spirit? If someone were to come into the inner sanctuary of my life as into my home would they find more evidence that sin lives there than signs of the Spirit living there?

KINDLING QUOTE

"See how he drives the devils from the souls of men, as we the wolves from our sheep folds!"

DAY 10

Virgil said, "In each and every man a god dwells." An old rabbinical saying illuminates this further by adding that it is not the passing guest who is master of the house, but the one who lives there as a permanent resident. That master is either sin (Romans 7.17,20) or the Spirit (John 14.17). It is not enough to have occasional bursts of goodness while maintaining a life-style (openly or secretly) of self-pleasing passions and impulses.

Paul uses yet another image in 1 Corinthians 3.16. There he likens the Christian's life to a holy temple when he asks: "Don't you know that you yourselves are God's temple and that God's Spirit lives in you?" And then he adds the direst of dire warnings, "If anyone destroys God's temple, God will destroy him; for God's temple is sacred, and you are that temple." (v.17)

Keep these things in mind as you read the parable Jesus gave in Matthew 12.43-45.

FIRESTARTER VERSE

Those who obey his commands live in him, and he in them. And this is how we know that he lives in us: we know it by the Spirit he gave us (I John 3.24)

And if anyone does not have the Spirit of Christ, he does not belong to Christ (8.9b)

DAY 11

I recall that, during a mission to Horley, near Gatwick Airport, the minister of the Baptist Church, and I made a visit to a gypsy site. Remembering that there had been quite a strong spiritual revival among the travellers, I asked the young lad who met us at the entrance whether there were any Christians in residence.

He cheerfully assured us that everyone on that small encampment were believers and asked if we were too. After assuring him that we were, I was rather surprised by his next question. "Are you full of the Holy Spirit?" he quizzed.

I affirmed that we were but wondered what he meant by the question. Did he mean, as is so often the case, do you speak in tongues? The answer would then have been no. I would have been in good company in the early church for Paul asks, "Do all speak in tongues?" The context demands the answer "no", without making a judgement on whether a person has or has not the Spirit of Christ.

Indeed, a person may speak in tongues and display other even greater powers and not be filled with the Spirit. Jesus Himself warned of the many who would say on the day of judgement, "Lord, Lord, did we not prophesy in your name, and in your name drive out demons and perform many miracles? But he will dismiss them with the devastating words, 'I never knew you. Away from me, you evildoers!'" (Matthew 7.22-23)

True believers, as opposed to church-goers, should never be divided between those who have the Spirit and those who do not. All who are in Christ have His Spirit in them. A church-goer, on the other hand, may or may not be a Christian. One who has been baptized as a child or even as an adult may not be a Christian. Neither confirmation, nor mere verbal profession, nor any external attachment or ritual act can of itself confer salvation or guarantee whether a person be Christian. All Christians, however, have this in common: they all have the Spirit of Christ. If someone does not, he or she would not belong to Christ.

How then shall a person know if he is a Christian? How may we distinguish between those who are truly filled with the Spirit of Christ and those who are guilty of counterfeit? (2 Thessalonians 2.9)

KINDLING QUOTE

"He is our Lord and Master, Elder Brother, King, Saviour, The Divine Man, the human God. To believe in him is to give ourselves up to him in obedience - to search out his will and to do it."

DAY II

The answer lies in obedience to Christ, as He was obedient to the Father. This does not mean we shall win every battle with our own sin but we shall know on whose side we are fighting in the war against sin. It is possible that this is what Paul had in mind in this very verse when having already spoken of the indwelling Spirit of God, he talks of having the Spirit of Christ. What was the Spirit of Christ if it were not that power to overcome sin in complete obedience to the Father? Therefore, those who truly belong to Christ Jesus are the ones who have put to death and "... crucified the sinful nature with its passions and desires." (Galatians 5:24)

Ours is not to judge others but to examine ourselves to see whether we are really in the faith (2 Corinthians 13:5). As you read Luke chapter 7, ask God to show you what you must do today.

FIRESTARTER VERSE

This is how we know who the children of God are ... Anyone who does not do what is right is not a child of God.
(I John 3.24)

Cedric Thumbleweed experiences a sudden vague uncertainty that his methods of spiritual progress may not in fact be sufficient.

But if Christ is in you, your body is dead because of sin, yet your spirit is alive because of righteousness (8.10)

DAY 12

Though Paul presumes he is writing his letter to believers in Rome, he shows studied sensitivity in his choice and qualification of pronouns. In the previous verse he uses the general term "if anyone", because he is talking of those who have not the Spirit of Christ. Now that he has returned to the more positive, indeed opposite statement, he says "if you". But note the "if". We do well to contemplate that two-letter word and its implications until we can say with unpresumptuous certainty "as" - as Christ is in me.

At such time as Christ is in the believer there are two consequences. The one death, the other life.

Death of the body or death in the body? The apostle is unusually vague on this point. He may be referring to his explanation of why sin brought death to all in his Adam thesis. "Therefore", he argued, "just as sin entered the world through one man, and death through sin, and in this way death came to all men, because all sinned" (5.12). Moffatt's paraphrase of today's text captures this idea well, "If Christ is within you, though the body is a dead thing owing to Adam's sin."

This would certainly fit the context and by inserting the word "though", which is quite legitimate in the original Greek text, he overcomes what some may see as a problem of Christians being called dead.

But dead they most certainly are, not only in the Adamic sense, that because of sin all die, but also in the Pauline sense of the Christian dying with Christ. This is how he put it, "For we know that our old self was crucified with him ..." (6.6) This too would fit the context especially as that verse goes on to talk of the body of sin being rendered powerless, which it is, if Christ has dealt with it on the cross. It can no longer condemn. Every true believer in the spiritual sense has already died, ready to be raised to a new life in the Spirit.

The question arises, in the second half of this verse, as to whether the Spirit is "your spirit" or the "Holy Spirit".

KINDLING QUOTE

"When a man says, 'I did wrong; I hate myself and the deed; I cannot endure to think that I did it!' then, I say, is atonement begun. Without that, all that the Lord did would be lost."

DAY 12

The N.I.V. has plumped for "your spirit", which may indeed be right, but the Greek simply says "the Spirit". The Spirit throughout Romans 8 is the "Holy Spirit", even in verse 16 where Paul does talk of "our spirits" it is THE SPIRIT who bears witness with our spirits. In verse 9 he said, "... the Spirit of God lives in you" and also "... the Spirit of Christ". In the very next verse it is "the Spirit" who raised Christ from the dead, "living in you". Therefore, I am inclined to the view that the Spirit of God, the Spirit of Christ, the Holy Spirit is the life in you because of Righteousness. That is Christ's righteousness by which we are justified and in which we are called to holiness.

Consider this as you read 1 Peter 4.1-11.

FIRESTARTER VERSE

May God himself, the God of peace, sanctify you through and through. May your whole spirit, soul and body be kept blameless at the coming of our Lord Jesus Christ.
(1 Thessalonians 5.23)

And if the Spirit of him who raised Jesus from the dead is living in you, he who raised Christ from the dead will give life to your mortal bodies through his Spirit, who lives in you (8.11)

DAY 13

Paul finely balances his terms in this verse. Jesus was raised in the sense of being awakened, in much the same way as we might say, "it's time to get up". This does not mean that He was not dead, but that His body had not been subject to decay. When He was raised the tomb was empty. The body that had been there was there no more. It was a bodily resurrection.

On the other hand, when he talks of believers' resurrection, he uses a word meaning "to give life" or "to restore life", because for us, the resurrection is the fulfilment of His gift of eternal life. We rightfully deserved death but He has given us life if the Spirit is in us.

This life is a present reality - "the Spirit living in you" - and a future promise - "will give life to your mortal bodies". It is the "new life" Paul has been speaking of in chapter 6 in relation to baptism, where he says, "We were therefore buried with him through baptism into death" - symbolised by going under the water - "in order that, just as Christ was raised from the dead ..." - symbolised by coming up out of the water - "we too may live a new life." (v.4)

Clearly, by "new life", he meant a new life now. A present reality. A life controlled by the Holy Spirit through spiritual re-birth. (John 3.5-6) But it also includes the promise that these mortal bodies will be resurrected at the last because of re-birth by the Holy Spirit.

Paul may well have used the term "mortal bodies" to dispel any possibility of misunderstanding the content of the gospel. Already there were some, especially in Corinth, who were questioning not the resurrection of Christ, but their own physical resurrection. They were too close to the clear proofs and witness of those who saw the risen Christ to doubt that He was raised, but how could bodies which had decayed even to dust be reconstituted into their former state at the resurrection?

Paul answers this question in 1 Corinthians 15 which, even though it is a longer passage than usual, you would do well to read in its entirety.

KINDLING QUOTE

"This life, this eternal life, consists for a man in absolute oneness with God and all divine modes of being, oneness with every phrase of right and harmony."

DAY 13

As you do so, note how the apostle lists the consequences for not believing in the promise of a resurrection life for believers. In effect he says, if you cannot believe in the resurrection, your Christian faith is no faith at all. It is merely a delusion. You are left with an empty Christ because if He was not raised from the dead there is no ultimate proof of His deity. Paul had said in Romans 1.4 that Christ was "declared with power to be the Son of God BY HIS RESURRECTION FROM THE DEAD".

If Christ is not who He claimed to be then everything else comes tumbling down and we are left with mere tales and an empty message, empty faith, empty gospel and an empty hope.

But, Hallelujah! Christ is risen. And so will all be risen who put their trust and hope in Him.

FIRESTARTER VERSE

.. everyone who looks to the Son and believes in him shall have eternal life, and I will raise him up at the last day
(John 6.40)

Therefore, brothers, we have an obligation - but it is not to the sinful nature, to live according to it. For if you live according to the sinful nature, you will die; but if by the Spirit you put to death the misdeeds of the body, you will live (8.12-13)

DAY 14

As father and son were journeying in a car one day, in through the open window flew a bumble bee. The lad began to panic because, highly allergic to bee stings, he knew his life was in danger. Quietly, calmly, his father reached out and caught the bee in his hand. But after clenching his fist he opened his hand and let the bee escape. Before the boy had time to panic again he showed his son the black stinger implanted in his hand and said, "Look, son, it can't hurt you. I've got its stinger."

In reading Romans chapter 12 today, you will see that gratitude is the basis for a new life-style of holiness. It is precisely because the sting has been taken out of death that we surrender our bodies to God's will and purpose.

You know that whenever Paul says "therefore" you must look back to see what it is there for. Equally, whenever he uses the term "brothers", you know he is about to say something either deeply personal or very important. Here he starts with both, "therefore brothers."

As we look back we see that he has not only climaxed his teaching on the Spirit-filled life but has also completed a whole section which stretched right back to chapter 6 verse 1. There he had asked the question, in view of God's saving grace in Jesus Christ, "Shall we go on sinning so that grace may increase?"

The answer shows the enormous cost God has paid to rescue us through Christ, who alone overcame sin and death, and by the Holy Spirit freed us from its controlling power. We are, therefore, debtors, under obligation to God to live for him and no longer for His enemy - sin.

There is nothing gentle about his warning. It is kill or be killed! It is like the message of Moses to Israel, one of "life and death, blessings and curses." (Deuteronomy 30:15-20) At stake is not a land but a kingdom, not a nation but eternal life.

The warning is given to believers - "brothers". It is to "brothers" in another province, that of Galatia, that he says, "Do not be deceived: God cannot be mocked. A man reaps what he sows. The one who sows to please the sinful nature, from that nature will reap destruction; the one who sows to please the Spirit, from the Spirit will reap eternal life." (Galatians 6.7-8)

KINDLING QUOTE

"By acting upon what he sees and knows, hearkening to every whisper, obeying every hint of good, following whatever seems light, man will at length arrive."

DAY 14

Paul is not playing theological games when he says, "you will die". He means it. He is emphatic. Even for himself he says, "I beat my body and make it my slave so that after I have preached to others, I myself will not be disqualified for the prize." (1 Corinthians 9.27)

The difference between the believer and the unbeliever is the Spirit. It is "by the Spirit" that we put to death the misdeeds of the body. Both here, and in Colossians 3.5 the tense is present; which indicates a constant continuous action on the part of the believer and the Spirit in the believer. Never forget that Ephesians 2.8 and 9 is followed by Ephesians 2.10! Kill the sin, live for His glory.

FIRESTARTER VERSE

Blessed are those who hunger and thirst for righteousness, for they will be filled (Matthew 5.6)

Because those who are led by the Spirit of God are sons of God (8.14)

DAY 15

The first thirteen verses of this chapter have been a wild roller-coaster, sometimes reaching dizzy heights only to be plunged to desolate depths. Paul has elevated the Spirit of God against the sin-nature. White-knuckled, we plunge downwards with tightened stomachs, only to be launched upward to ecstatic gratitude as conflict has given way to peace, guilt to forgiveness, death to life and judgement to resurrection. We have only been shown hell in order that we might appreciate heaven.

We get off the wild machine not at some midway point between the two but at the very apex. The antithesis between the Spirit and the flesh gives way to the harmony between the Spirit of God and the sons of God. Just as Jesus, the eternal Son of God, lived to do only the will of His Father, so we are to be those led by the Spirit into the obedience of sonship.

How shall we be led? How shall we know that it is the Holy Spirit and not some other? Primarily, by the word of God in its written form, the Scriptures. The Holy Spirit prompted men to speak God's word (2 Peter 1.21). As Paul says elsewhere, "All Scripture is God-breathed and is useful for teaching, rebuking, correcting and training in righteousness, so that the man (or woman) of God may be thoroughly equipped for every good work." (2 Timothy 3.16)

Another way is by seeing where He leads. The inner-prompting and conviction that the Spirit of God brings is not at variance with His word. We know, for instance, that obedience leads to righteousness (6.16). Therefore, the Spirit will not lead a son or daughter of God into sin, even on the pretext that the end justifies the means.

He will not lead a believer to do anything which does not bear the fruit of love, joy, peace, patience, kindness, goodness, faithfulness, gentleness and self-control, because a tree is known by its fruit. (Galatians 5.22; Matthew 7.16)

KINDLING QUOTE

"To do what we ought, as children of God, is an altogether higher, more divine, more potent, more creative thing, than to write the grandest poem, paint the most beautiful picture, carve the mightiest statue, build the most magnificent temple, dream out the most enchanting symphony."

DAY 15

Thirdly, He will not lead you to do anything you have not seen in Jesus. Every action, every word, every motive, every virtue you have seen in Jesus is itself a demonstration of true sonship. He is our Divine Older Brother who, knowing the character, authority and glory of the Father, has chosen to please Him in every way. Even though the Spirit led Him into the wilderness of temptation, He went to confront sin and the devil himself, armed only with the word and obedient submission to His Father.

You may read about this in Luke 4.1-13 and, as you do, ask the Holy Spirit to lead you through the temptations of today in victory and sonship.

...known by its fruit

FIRESTARTER VERSE

**But when he, the Spirit of truth, comes, he will guide you into all truth
(John 16.13)**

For you did not receive a spirit that makes you a slave again to fear, but you received the Spirit of sonship (8.15)

DAY 16

As a baby, I was deserted by my mother at the death of my father. For the next ten years I lived in a Southampton children's home. Often confused by the petty rules and restrictions of personal freedom, I rebelled against what I perceived to be a harsh and unloving environment.

Imagine my elation when one Christmas-time I was told that my dream had come true. Foster parents had been found and I was to become their son. They loved me well enough and tried so hard to show me how much, but the behaviour patterns established throughout my formative years were still in place. Much as I loved them, I could not believe they could love me. I stole from them and resumed my old habits of house-breaking. Before long I was right back where I started, in the children's home with all its cold regimentation, until the day I left school.

The taste and warmth of unconditional love, which I had never known before, seemed all the more remote now that I had lost it.

Paul's great pastoral heart sees this very danger. Those who had formerly been slaves to the legalism of the written code and the law of sin and death were now adopted as sons of God Himself. The fear of death and punishment which held them in bondage had not been broken only to be replaced by a greater fear of retribution. Any warnings Paul has given in the previous verses are but to show where they have come from in order that the new relationship may be fully appreciated.

Christ Jesus has paid the penalty for all that is past. The Holy Spirit has come to deliver us from bondage to old habits and give power for the new life in the present. Our Father may be fully trusted to love us to the last because "There is no fear in love. But perfect love drives out fear, because fear has to do with punishment." (1 John 4.18)

Sons may choose to be slaves, not to fear, but to willing service. Jesus the Son of God chose to become a slave, in order that we, the slaves of sin and death, might become the sons of God (Philippians 2.7). Little wonder then that Paul should delight to call himself "a servant of Christ Jesus" - more literally a slave (*doulos*) of Christ Jesus. We ourselves are called to be willing "slaves of righteousness" (6.18-19) as we become slaves of "the new way of the Spirit."

KINDLING QUOTE

"His perfection is his love. All his divine rights, his power, his justice, his righteousness, his mercy, his fatherhood - every divine attribute we think to ascribe him - rests upon his love. God's love is what he is."

DAY 16

What of those who have fallen back into sin? Will God do less than my foster parents, to whom in later years I became no longer a confused child but a devoted son? The way back to God is much shorter than the distance travelled away from Him. As short as a prayer. Abba, Father.

This seems like a good time to re-read the story of the Loving Father in Luke 15.11-32. As you do this ask yourself what Jesus, our older brother, would have done for the prodigal son.

FIRESTARTER VERSE

For God did not give us a spirit of timidity, but a spirit of power, of love and self-discipline (2 Timothy 1.7)

And by him we cry, 'Abba', Father (8.15b)

DAY 17

No-one reading Romans as a whole could avoid the conclusion that uppermost in the mind of its writer is the transition between the Old Covenant of law and the New Covenant of grace. Inevitably, as his pen hovered over the page at this point, he was overwhelmed by a single Aramaic word - 'Abba'. In that one word, the old and the new covenant would kiss each other and make both complete.

From the Garden of Eden to the Garden of Gethsemane, this 'Abba' Father had heard the cries of His children. Abel's blood had cried out to Him from the ground (Genesis 4.10). The cry of Sarah's empty womb had moved Him, and no less, the cries of Ishmael had reached His ears (Genesis 16 and 21.17). Was Moses not adopted by more than Pharaoh's daughter when 'Abba' heard a cry from the bulrushes? (Exodus 2.6)

Most significant of all, a cry was heard in heaven as the Israelites groaned under the yoke of Egypt. Their cry for help God heard (Exodus 2.24) and through His adopted Moses He said to Pharaoh, "Israel is my first-born son, ... Let my son go, so he may worship me." (Exodus 4.22,23)

How could the apostle write anything else? Release from the thrall of sin and death and slavery to a written code has been his very theme. If God could hear the cries of Israel and act to free her, how much more would he hear the cry of His only un-adopted Son as He cried from the garden 'Abba', Father. (Mark 14.36)

It is very doubtful whether a person has ever come into a conscious relationship with God without at least a cry of thanksgiving and worship. It is certain that never a cry from one of His children has been lost or fallen on deaf ears. He who heard the cry 'forgive me' will as surely hear every cry of His adopted ones. There is no loneliness that He will not share. There is no heartache that He will not care about. There is no grief to leave Him unmoved, nor despair left unsoothed. God is your Father, He hears your cry and even your whimper, your sob or your sigh. The very intimacy of the name by which Jesus addressed His Father is the closeness of His love to all who dare to call Him 'Abba'.

Two other Aramaic words are with us to this day and both are an appropriate response to this, the most precious word in any language. They are Hallelujah and Amen.

KINDLING QUOTE

"There is a live heart at the centre of the lovely order of the universe - a heart to which all the rest is but a clothing form - a heart that bears every truthful thought, every help-needing cry of each of its children, and must deliver them."

DAY 17

NOW LISTEN, MAVIS, I THINK I'VE GOT THE RESOURCES TO HANDLE THIS — I MEAN, WHAT DID GOD GIVE US BRAINS FOR...?

I JUST FANCIED A LITTLE PRAYER!

One of the surest ways of knowing whether you are a child of God is your desire to come to Him as Abba, Father, in prayer and praise. I do not mean that will always be easy, or that you will even know what to say, but the Spirit will always usher a true son or daughter into the presence of the Father. The person who never prays is a practical atheist.

Come now to the Garden as you read Mark 14.22-36.

FIRESTARTER VERSE

I will be a Father to you, and you will be my sons and daughters, says the Lord Almighty (2 Corinthians 6.18)

The Spirit himself testifies with our spirit that we are God's children (8.16)

DAY 18

I am told that the original of William Hogarth's portrait of Captain Coram is to be found in London's Foundling Hospital and one day I hope to see it. The great satirical artist of the early 18th century could, if he chose, use his palette and brush to reduce the constitutionally vain to objects of ridicule and pity. But not so Coram. It is said that this was the best Hogarth ever painted.

Coram was the founder of a hospital for homeless children. He had used all of his own considerable fortune and worked with such diligence in acts of charity that eventually his own health suffered. In those days there was no retirement pension and so friends made a collection for him. When this was presented to him he said, "I did not waste the wealth I possessed in self-indulgence or vain expense, and am not ashamed to own that in my old age I am poor."

Hogarth's portrait bears its own testimony to this man who though uncommonly rough and forbidding in the flesh is portrayed with an expression of "natural dignity and great benevolence".[1] He had apparently caught the inner-man.

We may never have our picture hung, nor words of praise written or said about us. What we are, and what we do that is of God may go unnoticed, or worse, be cynically misrepresented. Never mind. There is a witness who certifies that we are the children of God. He - the Holy Spirit - does this for the sake of our own assurance.

Have you noticed how, in doing this, our Father God treats us like His own Son Jesus. When He was baptised the Holy Spirit came upon Him in the form of a dove and a voice came from heaven saying, "You are my Son, whom I love; with you I am well pleased." (Luke 3.22b)

God's witness to us is with our own inner spirit, because it is not for the sake of others but for our own assurance of acceptance and salvation. It is because we need to know personally that we are the children of God.

> KINDLING QUOTE
>
> "Fatherhood and sonship are one, except that fatherhood looks down lovingly, and sonship looks up lovingly. Love is all."

---

[1] Allan Cunningham, *Lives of the Most Eminent Briitsh Painters, Sculptors and Architects*, John Murray (London 1829.)

DAY 18

The testimony of the Spirit does touch the emotions. But if it were only emotional there may be a danger of self-delusion. This is why Paul has given other criteria by which our spirits may verify the inner conviction. The whole of Romans chapter 8 is about confidence and hope. Everything between the "No condemnation" of verse one and "no separation" at the end is to assure the child of God that he/she is accepted "warts and all". He has talked, as we have seen, of a mind-set on what the Spirit desires, which brings life and a tangible peace of heart and mind. (vs.5,6) He has talked about a life-style of disciplined self-control; an active putting to death of bad behaviour (vs.13,14). This life-style, and of course, the promises of Scripture itself, confirm by emotion, by thought and by conduct that we are children of God, confident of His Fatherhood.

As you read 1 Peter 1, stop for a few moments at verse 13 and think of what that word 'hope' means to you.

FIRESTARTER VERSE

How great is the love the Father has lavished upon us, that we should be called the children of God!
(1 John 3.1)

Now if we are children, then we are heirs - heirs of God and co-heirs with Christ (8.17a)

DAY 19

KINDLING QUOTE

"Our childhood is born from his Fatherhood."

According to Roman law, a person adopted into a new family took on the full rights of that family and in effect started a brand new life. All old debts were cancelled, but at the same time any property or goods brought into the family became the property of the family. The new father exercised full rights of discipline, but in return all the privileges and benefits including inheritance were his or hers as though by right of birth.

This is clearly what Paul has in mind for the believer. That which belonged to Israel as a birthright is now given to even Gentile Christians. The apostle has been laying the foundation for this statement throughout the letter and in chapters nine to eleven expands on the theme as it relates specifically to the Jews, as it were, the older brother. But here the apostle wants to show that the pattern established with Israel merely foreshadowed God's greater plan.

God had been with Israel but by His Spirit He would be in the believer (v9). As they were called to righteousness so must we be righteous (12-13). As they were led out of Egypt into the promised land so we are His children by adoption. And just as they were heirs of the Old Covenant so all who are His children, whether Jew or Gentile, male or female, rich or poor, educated or simple, all are inheritors of His Kingdom in Christ.

For the Jews, the inheritance was a matter of the promised land. The Psalmist sums up their expectation when he says, "the righteous will inherit the land and dwell in it forever." (Psalm 37.29) The Christian inheritance is all of God as Father and everything He has given to His own son, Jesus.

Our share, then, is not just with Israel but with Christ Himself - He whom the writer to Hebrews calls "the heir of all things". (Hebrews 1.2)

Have you caught the impact of that? All that God has prepared for His own Son is yours and mine if we are the children of God. We shall not wait for Him to die in order to receive it because God will never die - He is the inheritance. Strangely, it is we who die. Firstly we die to self and then at the end of our days we die physically and at the resurrection enter into our full inheritance.

DAY 19

A portion of that inheritance is already ours. We shall enjoy Him forever but while here on earth we have Him in the Holy Spirit who is, as Paul says, "a deposit guaranteeing our inheritance until the redemption of those who are God's possession". (Ephesians 1.14) This is surely easy enough to understand. A son may be privy to the content of his father's will and know what he will one day receive. One day the estate may be his. In the meantime his father may choose to give him a portion of what he has to set him up in business or help him with some expense.

Jesus had much to say about our inheritance. Read Matthew 19.16-30, to see how one man turned away from it.

FIRESTARTER VERSE

If you belong to Christ, then you are Abraham's seed, and heirs according to promise (Galatians 3.29)

If indeed we share in his sufferings in order that we may also share in his glory (8.17b)

DAY 20

In John Bunyan's *Pilgrim's Progress*, Christiana has just expressed a wish that she and her children be carried over into the presence of the King. To which the angel (Visitor) replies, "Christiana, the bitter comes before the sweet. The only way to enter Celestial City is to go the same way that your husband took before you, through the wicket-gate ahead." She would have to face the same trials that Christian before her had endured.

The giants of "Despair" and "Assault Lane" were nothing new to Bunyan who for twelve years languished in a Bedfordshire Prison because he preached the gospel outside the State Church of England during the persecution of dissenters in the mid-17th century. (We thank God in these days for the fellowship of believers across denominational lines.) The "Slough of Despond" and "Hill Difficulty", the "Valley of Humiliation" and even the spectre of the "Shadow of Death" were Bunyan's constant companions as he wrote that Christian classic. Evidently he empathised with the apostle Paul "in chains" and knew well the journey of suffering toward his share in glory.

More than a century later, Norway would have its own Bunyan in the person of Hans Nielsen Hauge. He too spent ten years in prison (1804-1814) for preaching the gospel all over the southern half of his country. Wherever he preached, revival broke out. But there too it was illegal to preach outside the State church, and in spite of his assistance to the poor in starting paper-mills and trading stations to provide employment, he was thrown into gaol.

To this day believers in many parts of the world risk imprisonment and even death for their faith. Most often, though, the persecution is either economic or verbal. I preached in a small Ukrainian town where a Baptist believer wished to plant a new church. When she was forced by strength of numbers to hire the public hall the local Orthodox priest complained to the new "Democratic" authorities. Not only were the ninety Baptists denied the right of hiring the hall but their leader was fired from her job working for the State.

KINDLING QUOTE

"It is vain to think that any weariness, however, caused, any burden, however slight, may be got rid of otherwise than by bowing the neck to the yoke of the Father's will."

DAY 20

In every age of history, Christians have suffered because of their faith. As Paul said to his young disciple Timothy, "In fact, everyone who wants to live a godly life in Christ Jesus will be persecuted". (2 Timothy 3.12) For him suffering was not just a mystical sympathy with Christ, and certainly not merely as an end in itself, but a necessary and inevitable path to glory. He testified, "I want to know Christ and the power of His resurrection and the fellowship of sharing in his suffering, becoming like him in his death." (Philippians 3.10)

How did Jesus put it? "If anyone would come after me, he must deny himself and take up his cross and follow me." (Mark 8.34) As you read his words in John 15 look out for the cost of discipleship but at the same time remember that "just as the sufferings of Christ flow over into our lives, so also through Christ our comfort overflows." (2 Corinthians 1.5)

FIRESTARTER VERSE

But rejoice that you participate in the sufferings of Christ, so that you may be overjoyed when his glory is revealed
(I Peter 4.13)

I consider that our present sufferings are not worth comparing with the glory that will be revealed in us (8.18)

DAY 21

Today there is good news. Do you ever feel you have more than your fair share of suffering? Has bereavement clouded your days or financial worries ruined your sleep? Has the dull ache of prolonged illness made the hours seem longer than their allotted minutes? Have you felt the heat of "fiery trials", persecution and victimization because of your faith? Has your confidence in the providence of God been worn thin by distressing events and broken relationships? Then, I repeat, today there is good news.

See how Paul personalizes this text. No room here for grand theories about why God allows suffering. His theology has been tempered by life's experience. It has been tested through hunger, beatings, ship-wrecks, imprisonments, slanderous accusations, deserting friends, sorrow, poverty, depression, chains and dishonour, to say nothing of his "thorn in the flesh". But he takes it all on the chin because he has made a calculation. After totting it all up and putting it in the scales it does not even begin to move the weight on the other side.

Elsewhere he calls them "light and momentary troubles" (2 Corinthians 4.17). He is not a masochist, nor is he merely advocating mind over matter. He has thought the issue through logically and spiritually and even given us a clue of the progression of his thinking. "Suffering produces perseverance," he argues, "perseverance, character, and character, hope." Therefore "we rejoice in the hope of the glory of God." (Romans 5.3). The "eternal glory" outweighs every discomfort, right on through to the worst torment that could ever be inflicted (2 Corinthians 4.17).

No wonder the scarred apostle urged believers to keep their hearts and minds fixed on things above "where Christ is seated at the right hand of God" (Colossians 3.1-4) because there is the goal; there is the prize.

KINDLING QUOTE

"My tomorrow, I mock you away! Shadowless nothing, thou! God's tomorrow, come, dear day, For God is in thee now."

DAY 21

Like an athlete, prepared to strain every fibre between the starting pistol and the tape ahead, we count whatever we are going through today as worth the effort.

THIS RACE BUSINESS IS A CINCH — WHO WANTS TO BE A FANATIC AND GO FOR THE PRIZE?

FIRESTARTER VERSE

Here is a trustworthy saying: if we died with him, we will also live with him; if we endure, we will also reign with him
(2 Timothy 2.11)

We live as those with great expectations. The nature of "the glory that will be revealed in us" and indeed for us is not yet fully known. We are like the heir to an estate who may guess at the extent of the fortune he has inherited but until the lawyer reads the details of the will, the precise details remain hidden. It will be revealed, of that neither Paul, nor we, need have any doubt. Not so much "pie in the sky when you die" as hope in the truth while you live. For the glory yet to be revealed exists, not only in the promise of God in the gospel, but also in the person of Christ already glorified who is coming again in glory. (Colossians 3.4)

See how the path to glory goes through the valley of suffering as you read 2 Corinthians 4.7-5.5.

The creation waits in eager expectation for the sons of God to be revealed (8.19)

DAY 22

Harold Wakeford is a landscape gardener. Perhaps because he has spent so much time tending and nursing nature, his face has taken on something of its rustic charm. More of a windswept gnarled oak than his own neatly manicured Surrey gardens, but no less attractive. His smile is like the wind bringing to life a wheat field. Still his charactered but aging eyes dance like lambs out to impress a spring morning.

Harold has such a bee in his bonnet about the wonders of creation that to hear him talk about it you would swear he was God's own gardener. If he has a gripe at all, it is that we who presume to speak on behalf of God rarely ever talk about the non-human part of what God has made.

This morning Harold will smile. But even he, who sees weeds as merely flowers in the wrong place at the wrong time, would readily concede that creation is itself suffering under the legacy of human sin. It is not just that pollution, deforestation and over-population have created global warming, decimation of fauna and flora and the poisoning of food chains, though these must surely be the latest signs of our human madness. It goes further back than the Industrial Revolution to the very beginning of what we foolishly call "The Ascent of Man" but which theologians more accurately call "the fall".

When Adam sinned God said, "Cursed is the ground because of you". (Genesis 3.17) There is a matching brokenness, a synergy of destruction, between the last of God's creation and all that is and draws life in the cosmos. Isaiah prophesies that the Lord is going to lay waste the earth and devastate it, because "the earth is defiled by its people; they have disobeyed the laws, violated the statutes and broken the everlasting covenant." (See Isaiah 24)

In this verse Paul personifies nature as an innocent victim, a passive prisoner suffering the consequences of human sin and longing for release and restoration to its former glory.

KINDLING QUOTE

"Draw near Sun of Righteousness, and make the trees burgeon, and the flowers blossom, and the voices grow mellow and glad, so that all shall join in praising thee, and find thereby that harmony is better than unison."

DAY 22

He uses a compound of three Greek words to paint a picture. *Apo* means "from far away" or "away from". *Kapa* is the word for "head" and *dokeo* is a verb used to say "watching out" or "waiting for something". The whole word *apokapadokia* literally means "stretching the head forward in eager expectation waiting for something to come from a fixed point on the horizon. In fact J. B. Phillips translates this verse "The whole creation is on tiptoe to see the wonderful sight of the sons of God coming into their own." Like prisoners of war anticipating liberation, the creation is like a man standing on tiptoe straining forward with an eager longing.

It is waiting for that time when Christ shall come "to bring all things in heaven and on earth together under one head". (Ephesians 1.10) At that time the true believers, the sons of God, will be revealed in their true sanctified nature and break the curse of Adam to form a new solidarity between man and nature. Then the trees of the field shall clap their hands and so will Harold.

Now read Isaiah 35 and stand on tiptoe with the creation.

FIRESTARTER VERSE

You will go out in joy and be led forth in peace; the mountains and hills will burst into song before you, and all the trees of the field will clap their hands (Isaiah 55.12)

For the creation was subjected to frustration, not by its own choice, but by the will of the one who subjected it, in hope (8.20)

DAY 23

> *Oh! Why did God creator wise*
> *That peopled highest Heaven*
> *With spirits masculine, create at last*
> *This novelty on earth, this fair defect*
> *Of Nature?*

John Milton's question finds an answer in the title of the epic poem which contains it. *Paradise Lost* may well be the best commentary on the opening clause of this text.

Who has not at some time questioned the contradiction of nature? The peaceful serenity of snow-capped mountains on a spring morning contrasting the anger of an ash-spewing volcano in destructive mode. The majesty, mirth and marvel of the animal kingdom so innocently tender and inquisitive, yet "red in tooth and claw". It is only out of the conquest of blight, mildew and bind-weed that horticulture triumphs and gardens boast their blazing colours. Why does that same sun bring life, splendour and comfort to many while at the same time dealing death in the desert?

It was not always so. There was a time of no contradiction, when God Himself looked and saw that it was good. It was into this primal perfection that the creator planted an innocent couple, man and woman. The rest, as they say, is history. These who had been commissioned to rule over Paradise ruined it by their ingratitude. Instead of praising God with ecstatic appreciation for the wonder of all He had given, they were tempted to covet and have that one forbidden fruit.

Humans lost their innocence and brought a curse upon themselves. But not only upon themselves. All of creation came under God's curse (Genesis 3.17) so that nature would retain enough of God's stamp to remind us of God (Romans 1.20) and enough of death to remind us of our sin.

Nature had no choice in the matter. It became the innocent victim locked into the fallen world of mankind. Its suffering is not of its own making.

KINDLING QUOTE

"Flowers live. They come from the same heart as man himself, and are sent to be his companions and ministers."

DAY 23

When earthquakes shake foundations and hurricanes blast their fury, when viruses strike their deadly blow and bacteria invade, we do well to remember those other words of Milton,

> *Accuse not nature,*
> *she hath done her part;*
> *do thou but thine.*

Her destiny is tied in solidarity to that of the church, for her hope and head is the same - her creator and our Lord Jesus Christ are one. Isaiah's promise of a re-creation of heaven and earth (Isaiah 65.17) finds its fulfilment initially in Christ, as the work on the cross not only effects our salvation but also reconciles "all things" back to God.

Compare Isaiah 24 1-9 with the promises of Psalm 96 and give thanks. Stop and smell the roses!

Accuse not nature,

FIRESTARTER VERSE

Let the rivers clap their hands, let the mountains sing together for joy; let them sing before the Lord, for he comes to judge the earth (Psalm 98.8-9)

That the creation itself will be liberated from its bondage to decay and brought into the glorious freedom of the children of God (8.21)

DAY 24

Paul has daringly personified the sub-human creation as one looking forward in eager anticipation of the end-time revealing of the sons of God. (v19) Unabashed, he has shown how this innocent third party to the human fall was cursed to a futility now dramatized as "bondage to decay". But who could have foreseen that in three verses the writer would reach this, the very pinnacle of creation's place in God's plan of redemption?

Ironically, it is in a chapter pre-eminently concerned with the confident assurance of the believer that the clearest of all Biblical statements is given regarding the destiny of the cosmos. Its future hope is inextricably tied to that of the believer. Its bondage was in time past a direct result of human sin; its freedom in time to come will be a consequence of the deliverance of believers from sin to sonship. The hope of the children of God is the hope of all things.

What then will happen to the created order? There are clues to be found throughout Scripture which seem to show a parallel history and a mirrored destiny. For example, bondage is a common experience. We have been in "slavery to sin, law and death". Nature is trapped by the second law of thermodynamics that all things tend toward their own destruction, death and decay. This does not mean there is no beauty, order and life in nature any more than sinful persons are completely bereft of goodness. It simply means that both are bound by destructive forces which will ultimately lead to death.

Death for the believer and the cosmos is but a prelude to resurrection. The earth as we know it will pass away. (1 Corinthians 7.31) Scientists and the Scriptures agree that this passing will be by fire (2 Peter 3.10) But what then? It will be a new heaven and a new earth. But does this mean a new order of creation? I believe it does (Revelation 21.1) Surely the hope of every believer is to be gloriously freed from the body and its dogged inclination to sin by receiving at the resurrection a new body no longer enslaved to the law of sin and death. It is immortal and imperishable only because there is no more sin to bring it to death.

KINDLING QUOTE

"And then I thought how the sun, at the furthest point from us, had begun to come back toward us, looked upon us with a hopeful smile, and was like the Lord when He visited His people as a little one of themselves, to grow upon the earth until it should blossom as the rose in the light of His presence."

DAY 24

I therefore incline to the belief that the "reconciliation of all things" by Christ's death on the cross literally means all things - the whole sub-human creation and all who believe. There would surely be no "eager expectation" and "hope" if annihilation was its fate. No! Call it what you will, re-creation, reconstruction, why not resurrection? If our fortunes are so bound together, the perishable earth must be clothed with the imperishable (1 Corinthians 15.54) Eternal glory for the new heaven and new earth will then be for both deliverance from the now into an incorruptible never-ending perfection. Gone will be decay and presumably the second law of thermodynamics will give way to a higher law of life.

Isaiah 11.1-9 may give further clues into God's amazing plan.

FIRESTARTER VERSE

But in keeping with his promise we are looking forward to a new heaven and a new earth, the home of righteousness (2 Peter 3.13)

We know that the whole creation has been groaning as in the pains of childbirth right up to the present time (8.22)

DAY 25

"Save the world - recycle your cans here" proclaimed the banner at the Pilton Pop Festival. Friends of the Earth, Greenpeace and other ecologically-sound activists rightly draw our attention to the unbounded madness of indiscriminate and greedy exploitation of the earth's finite resources by man the master. From the plundering of the rain forests to the poisoning of oceans we have overtaxed the environment which sustains us.

Whether through wilful extravagance or idle neglect, the planet seems to be writhing in pain. Little wonder that idealistic and frightened people become extremists. The resurgence of mysticism and idolatrous worship of "Mother Earth", while understandable as a reaction, is not the answer. Worshipping the created instead of the creator is part of the problem, not the solution. (Romans 1.22-25)

What is required is an intelligent management and conservation of the earth by those whose immediate survival is at stake. But even when this is done it will not of itself "save the world". The groaning of creation will continue and as with labour even intensify as the *eschaton* (last days) approaches. Even as the children of God cry out "Abba, Father", the whole of nature cries in a "symphony of sighs". Even as "we groan, longing to be clothed with our heavenly dwelling" (2 Corinthians 5.2) so the creation groans with pregnant expectation. This, then, is not the murmur of death but the precursor to life.

Within the Scripture the "birth pangs" or birth pains are consistently used to announce the *eschaton* - God's salvation at the end of the age. Hence in that great statement by Jesus concerning the signs of the end-time He talks of earthquakes in various places and famines as "the beginning of birth pains". (Matthew 24.8) The pain is not meaningless but full of hope as though nature could feel in her womb the kicking and the thriving of a new and a perfect universe about to emerge like a bursting spring. With all the expectation of a mother in the delivery room she longs to see that which she hopes for.

KINDLING QUOTE

"There is jubilance in every sunrise, a sober sadness in every sunset."

DAY 25

The unbeliever will scoff at this scenario as much as he ridicules "the creation" as an act of God. I am reminded of the atheist who, on entering the study of Johann Kepler the Christian astronomer, spied on the desk a splendid model of the globe. He asked Kepler, "Who made it?" Kepler relied, "It made itself." The atheist laughed and asked again who made it? Only to receive the same reply. When the atheist became angry Kepler said, "How strange. You look at this simple model and say somebody must have made it and yet you can see all the wonder and intricacy of nature and say it just happened." If a single human chromosome contains twenty billion separate pieces of information, enough to fill four thousand, five hundred page volumes all waiting to spring into action, what matter a universe waiting re-birth!

Read about that coming day in 1 Thessalonians 4.13 to 5.11.

FIRESTARTER VERSE

While we are in this tent we groan and are burdened, because we do not wish to be unclothed but to be clothed with our heavenly dwelling
(2 Corinthians 5.4)

...yet you can see all the wonder and intricacy of nature and say it just happened??

Not only so, but we ourselves, who have the firstfruits of the Spirit, groan inwardly as we wait eagerly for our adoption as sons (8.23a)

DAY 26

In verse 15 it appeared that believers were already children adopted into God's family and yet it seems here that adoption is still to become a reality at some point in the future. I may understand this better than most because of my childhood experience. Hollybrook Homes in Southampton was certainly not as harsh a regime as Dickens portrayed of Victorian workhouses but neither did it have the warmth of true family life. Like Oliver Twist, I longed for escape from institutional existence. Perhaps my fortunes would match his and I would be adopted by a rich uncle.

When eventually, after ten of the most formative years of my life, a postman and his wife offered to adopt me I was understandably ecstatic. There was an inevitable time-lag between the announcement of their intentions and the move to their home in Bitterne. On several weekends I was able to visit and get a taste of what it would be like. Sufficient in fact to make that gap more frustrating than all the years which had gone before. One day, however, my bags were packed for the last time and I moved into 52 Chatsworth Road, my new home with my new parents, Mr. & Mrs. Smeeth. The eager anticipation had become a reality.

The believer lives with this same tension. The child of God has both the promise and a taste of adoption. This is what Paul means when he talks of the firstfruits of the Spirit. The Spirit lives in the believer as a guarantee of what is yet to be. Just as each weekend spent with the Smeeths gave me increasing confidence that one day I would move in, so the gift of the Holy Spirit is the beginning of a process which will be completed at the resurrection. As Paul says elsewhere, "He (God) anointed us, set his seal of ownership on us, and put his Spirit in our hearts as a deposit, guaranteeing what is to come." (2 Corinthians 1.22)

In the meantime, between the down-payment and the completion, the environment of sin, suffering and death cannot be escaped. The believer, like the creation, is subjected to frustration. Every lapse into sin, every lost battle, every persecution reminds the child of God that he or she is not yet at home.

KINDLING QUOTE

"The refusal, and the inability, to look up to God as our Father, is the one central wrong in the whole human affair, the one central misery."

DAY 26

Now we see why Paul has used the vivid illustration of sub-human creation as a picture of what the adopted sons and daughters of God can expect while on earth. As the whole creation groans with the pains of childbirth so the Christian "groans inwardly" under the weight of temptation's insistent rattle. If it were not for the indwelling Spirit they would consider themselves no different from the unbeliever. It is this, along with the work of Christ upon the cross by which justification is assured, which causes the adopted ones to look forward even as creation does, with eager expectation.

Ephesians chapter 1 has much to say about this hope. Read it with thanksgiving and anticipation of what is yet to be.

FIRESTARTER VERSE

Our citizenship is in heaven. And we eagerly await a Saviour from there, the Lord Jesus Christ (Philippians 3.20)

The redemption of our bodies (8.23b)

DAY 27

Martin Luther is said to have had only two days on his calendar - "Today" and "That day". If so he had caught precisely the "Now - but not yet" dichotomy of the gap between the reception of the Holy Spirit - now - and the redemption of the body which is yet to happen.

This "now - but not yet" tension was brought out very clearly in yesterday's Bible reading from Ephesians chapter 1. Verse 7 states confidently, "In him (Jesus) we have redemption through his blood, the forgiveness of sins, in accordance with the riches of God's grace." And yet, seven verses later, "until the redemption" is thrust forward into the future. "Having believed," says Paul, "you were marked with a seal, the promised Holy Spirit, who is a deposit guaranteeing our inheritance until the redemption of those who are God's possession..." (v.13,14)

This has important consequences as we live in between-times. We are not now as we shall be then. At the resurrection, and only at the resurrection, shall we receive the full inheritance. Only then shall the believer be perfect. Only then shall there be "no more death or mourning or crying or pain..." (Revelation 21.4)

I recall an occasion when I was suffering an acute depression. A minister called at my home and said, "If you were really a Christian, you would not be as you are." What poppycock! We all, believers and unbelievers, live in a fallen world which is awaiting redemption. Sickness, whether mental, emotional or physical is our common lot. It is part and parcel of "our present suffering." (v.18)

KINDLING QUOTE

"No amount of wrongdoing in a child can ever free a parent from the divine necessity of doing all he can to deliver and liberate his child."

DAY 27

What then, you may ask, is the difference between a Christian, a pagan and an atheist? On the surface not much. All get sick because of an hostile environment. All sin to a greater or lesser extent. All come under attack at sometime in a world where conflict, prejudice and misunderstanding are endemic. All have to work hard at relationships and most have disappointments, heartaches and even betrayals along the way.

If one were to look at life-styles alone there may be little to choose between any. There are too many decent pagans and too many failing Christians to make comparisons.

We must never forget that it was of believers that Paul said "all have sinned and fall short of the glory of God." (Romans 3.23) Note the present continuous tense - "fall short".

What separates the Christian from the unbeliever is that the believer has begun living in the between-times of being "justified freely by his (God's) grace through the redemption that came by Christ Jesus" (Romans 3.24), and the expected "redemption of the body" when it passes through death to the resurrection. Then the perishable will be freed to become imperishable and the mortal redeemed to immortality.

The pagan and the atheist may likewise be saved by repenting. The same blood of Christ which paid the penalty for my sin will suffice to free them from bondage and darkness. They too may enter the between-times by receiving the firstfruit of the Spirit.

As you read Paul's prayer in Colossians 1.9-14 ask yourself the question, "What have I been redeemed (freed) from?"

FIRESTARTER VERSE

**Dear friends, now we are children of God, and what we will be has not yet been made known. But we know when he appears, we shall be like him, for we shall see him as he is
(I John 3.2)**

For in this hope we were saved. But hope that is seen is no hope at all. Who hopes for what he already has? (8.24a)

DAY 28

Every third hour the carillon of the Civic Centre clock in my home town chimes out above the noise of traffic the tune of a hymn written by an earlier resident of Southampton, Isaac Watts.

> *O God, our help in ages past,*
> *Our hope for years to come,*
> *Our shelter from the stormy blast,*
> *And our eternal home.*

The decision to have that tune probably had as much to do with the devastating bombing raids of the Second World War, which tore the heart out of the city, as it did with honouring our hymn writer. It would have been natural enough as the centre was being rebuilt to have looked forward with new hope.

It was Victor Frankl who, as a prisoner in a Nazi concentration camp, observed the deadly effect that a loss of hope had on his companions. He later wrote, "Any attempt to restore a man's inner strength had first to succeed in showing him some future goal." As Coleridge the poet expressed it, "Hope without an object cannot live."

For this reason, the apostle directs the believer to do much as Watts did in his hymn eighteen centuries later. Look back to the past to see what God has done and look forward in hope.

"In hope we were saved." The backwards glance finds fuller expression in chapter 5.1-5 where Paul says "we have been justified through faith .... we have gained access by faith .... God has poured out his love into our hearts by the Holy Spirit, whom he has given us." Hope therefore is not mere wishful thinking but based firmly in the nature and past activity of God on our behalf in Christ. Such is the confidence when he wrote to the Ephesian believers, " For it is by grace you have been saved, through faith - and this not from yourselves, it is the gift of God." (Ephesians 2.8)

Be that as it may, the apostle is conscious too of the danger of over-confidence which may lead a person into one of two sins - that of indifference or even recklessness in the matter of personal behaviour. You may read his answer to this in today's reading in Romans chapter 6.

KINDLING QUOTE

"Sad-hearted, be at peace: the snowdrop lies Buried in sepulchre of ghastly snow; But spring is floating up the southern skies, And darkling the pale snowdrop waits below."

DAY 28

The other peril is one of arrogant pride which assumes that we have all the inheritance now. He may even have been conscious of the spiritual snobbery in the very church at Corinth from which he wrote the letter to Rome.

Had they not got all the gifts of the Spirit? Were not all the benefits of the Kingdom in the here and now? What place has suffering in the life of a Spirit-filled believer?

To such he would say "we fix our eyes not on what is seen, but on what is unseen. For what is seen is temporary, but what is unseen is eternal." (2 Corinthians 4.18) "We live by faith, not by sight." (2 Corinthians 5.7)

There is more beyond the deposit of our present possession - the hope stored up for us in heaven. (Colossians 1.5) Our hope is in God past, present and future.

FIRESTARTER VERSE

**Though you have not seen him, you love him; and even though you do not see him now, you believe in him and are filled with an inexpressible and glorious joy
(1 Peter 1.8)**

But if we hope for what we do not yet have, we wait for it patiently (8.25)

DAY 29

Florence Chadwick had been the first woman to swim the English Channel in both directions. Buoyed up by a new challenge, she began swimming the Catalina Channel between the Island of that name and the Californian coast, a distance of some 21 miles. Millions watched on television that July morning in 1952 as she battled her way through the cold shark infested waters. Several times rifles had to be used to frighten away sharks which came perilously close.

Sixteen hours after she entered the water she was numb with cold and dispirited because fog blanketed the coastline. She gave up the struggle and was hauled aboard the accompanying boat. When eventually the fog lifted the beach could be seen - less than half a mile away. "If only I could have seen the land," she cried, "I could have kept going." Two months later she did. This time, even though once again fog obscured the land, she persevered until she walked up the Californian beach, having beaten all records.

At first sight it may appear that this illustration falls down because there seems to be quite a huge difference between the strenuous effort of Florence Chadwick and the apparent inactivity of waiting patiently. Not so. The Greek word *hypomone* is packed with robust vitality. It has in it more Bulldog than Labrador. Patience is too passive a word to do it justice. Tenacious endurance; persistent determination; hanging-in when the going gets tough; there is no wimpishness here. The Christian may groan inwardly but hope makes the timid brave and gives backbone to the spineless.

KINDLING QUOTE

"To know our faith is weak, is the first step toward its strengthening."

DAY 29

Whereas nature must suffer passively in her waiting, the Christian has a certain amount of choice, especially when the suffering is as a direct result of belonging to Christ. Avoidance is one such choice. The minister who told his Christian son not to put his head above the parapet at school to let anyone know he was a Christian, may have thought he was being a good father to protect his son from the persecution of what he termed "the classroom mafia", but he failed in the teaching of *hypomone*.

Another choice may be to fight back. Suppose that same minister had said to his son, "Listen my boy. The world is a tough place. When you get to this new school you will find that some of the lads react against you because you are a Christian. If they pick on you; do unto them first what you think they may do to you." That may have some merit in the worldly sense of toughening him up but it is not *hypomone*.

Christian *hypomone* accepts the suffering as part of the cost of discipleship. But it is not just stoicism which passively absorbs "the slings and arrows of outrageous fortune". Nor is it masochism which takes morbid delight in pain for its own sake. *Hypomone* is a courageous acceptance of suffering, whether inflicted deliberately by another or as a natural consequence of being one with creation, knowing that the pain and the effort will produce something worthwhile or result in some benefit.

In this case the prize is the unseen but nonetheless real inheritance promised in verse 17. You may read about the goal-orientated perseverance in Hebrews 10:19-39

FIRESTARTER VERSE

By standing firm you will save yourselves (Luke 21.19)

In the same way, the Spirit helps us in our weakness. We do not know what we ought to pray (8.26a)

DAY 30

What is our weakness? Is it sin? No, else Paul would surely have said weaknesses, plural. Is it our suffering (v. 18)? Possibly. But more likely it is either a) a reference to the previous verse, in which case it would mean (in the same way that you hold on tenaciously, persevering in your waiting in hope for what you do not see) the Holy Spirit comes to help you., or b) the weakness is that we do not know what to pray for as we wait patiently for the inheritance.

The latter is, I believe, the most likely because of the idea implicit in the previous verse of "holding on". In the "between-times" of coming to God and waiting for God, we are often tempted to give up, and though forced to cry "Abba, Father", it is merely a cry of frustration and sometimes desperation. We may even be tempted to give up praying altogether.

I am reminded of the story of the father who, when building a log cabin, watched his son struggling with a log which was patently too heavy for the boy to manage. But the lad was not a quitter. He just huffed and puffed and summoned all his might to move that log.

His father smiled and called over, "Tom, are you using all the strength you have on that log?"

"Yes, Dad," panted back the red-faced boy.

At this time father moved to the other end of the log, to that position where he could take most of the weight himself but without taking so much that there was none left for the lad to lift. "There," he said as he took the bulk of the weight upon himself, "You see. You weren't using all your strength. Together we can lift it."

When you are tempted to give up the struggle or to give up praying there is one who takes up your log. He is the Spirit of the one who said, "My yoke is easy and my burden is light." (Matthew 11.30)

KINDLING QUOTE

"He only awaits the turning of our face toward him."

DAY 30

The following doggerel was written by an unknown soldier during the American Civil War and it contains much truth.

> *I asked for strength that I might achieve;*
> *He made me weak that I might obey.*
> *I asked for health that I might do great things;*
> *He gave me grace that I might do better things.*
> *I asked for riches that I might be happy;*
> *I was given poverty that I might be wise.*
> *I asked for power that I might have the praise of men;*
> *I was given weakness that I might feel a need of God.*
> *I asked for all things that I might enjoy life;*
> *I was given life that I might enjoy all things.*
> *I received nothing I had asked for*
> *But was given all that I ever hoped for.*

As you read 2 Corinthians 12.1-10 you will discover that even the apostle did not even know what to pray for. He lamented "We do not know what we ought to pray for," so take heart.

FIRESTARTER VERSE

The Lord is my helper; I will not be afraid. What can man do to me (Hebrews 13.6)

But the Spirit himself intercedes for us with groans that words cannot express (8.26b)

DAY 31

KINDLING QUOTE

Do you ever dry up in prayer? Have you ever prayed, got up from your knees and thought - you hypocrite? You used words but they were only empty phrases; or worse you prayed nothing at all. It was not that you had nothing to pray for. You may even have interceded for others but when it came to praying for yourself there seemed to be no starting point. In short, have you ever thought to yourself, like Hamlet "My words fly up, my thoughts remain below. Words without thought never to heaven go."

Welcome to the club! Your president is he who writes to you now, and your fellow members are all around you. Every Christian experiences down days when they frankly do not even want to pray. For the vast majority prayer is at least a dull duty to be performed as a preface or an appendix to the real business of living. Sometimes out of sheer habit you may drop to your knees with so much you need to say but no words to express it.

Here is some good news. There are times when you thought you had prayed nothing, either with many words or silence. But not only was God there with you, the Holy Spirit in you did the praying for you. You may not have known it but God and the Holy Spirit were in deep prayer conversation for you.

Many years ago I was quite ill and under sedation. It is strange how at the times when you most need to pray for yourself you feel least inclined to do so. Day after day my wife, Sue, would sit on the bed and say, "Vic I'm going to pray for you." She did not just mean praying for me to get better - though she did that. What Sue meant was - I will pray for you the things I know you would be praying if you were better.

Love, of course, enables one to know the heart in this way. In the same way the Holy Spirit who poured love into our hearts (Romans 5.5) knows the deep wells of need and emotion. He sees the suffering Christian (v.18). He hears the "groans" of nature with its longing to be freed from imperfection (v.22). He listens to the "groans", the deep sighs, of the believer, waiting in hope for the redemption and resurrection. And would you believe it - joins in the groaning!

DAY 31

His groans are deeper than ours. There are no words in the vocabulary of any language to express what is on the heart of God for His darling creation and family of faith.

When we sin, it is Jesus who intercedes for us in heaven. John put it like this, "If anybody does sin, we have one who speaks to the Father in our defence - Jesus Christ, the Righteous One." (1 John 2.1) But when we are weak and vulnerable and do not even know what we want to say to God, it is not in heaven but from within that the Holy Spirit wings prayer heavenward for us. Better to have one such prayer with not a word spoken than the most eloquent outpouring of words but no prayer.

Ramon Lull tesified how God had spoken reassurance into his soul during a time of spiritual dryness. "You need not spek to me - only look toward me; for your eyes speak to my heart."[1]

As you read Ephesians 6.10-20 meditate on v.18 and ask God to show you what it means to "Pray in the Spirit."

FIRESTARTER VERSE

So do not fear, for I am with you; do not be dismayed, for I am your God. I will strengthen you and help you; I will uphold you with my righteous right hand.
(Isaiah 41.10)

---

[1] S.M. Zwemer, *The Solitary Throne*, Pickering & Inglis, 1937

And he who searches our hearts knows the mind of the Spirit (8.27a)

DAY 32

Who is it that searches our hearts? Exclusively God, for only he can. My wife says she can read me like a book. No doubt she knows me better than any other but even she does not know me as God does.... every thought, every motive, every grace, every sin, every experience from the womb till the present, and for all I know, even beyond. As the Psalmist has said, "O Lord, you have searched me and you know me." (Psalm 139.1)

We are so prone to make judgements based on the external factors such as appearance, wealth, position or power but God looks beneath the surface to things as they really are. When a person makes application for a job, a C.V. helps a prospective employer to make an assessment but it is flawed in so far as the applicant may reveal only that which gives the very best impression. References help but are only ever as good as the honesty and objectivity of the referee. Personality assessment and even lie-detectors may dig deeper but are only as good as the questions they ask.

When Samuel was told by God to anoint a new king for Israel he presumed that Eliab was God's obvious choice because of his appearance and height but the Lord had to remind his servant, "Do not consider his appearance or his height, for I have rejected him. The Lord does not look at the things man looks at. Man looks at the outward appearance, but the Lord looks at the heart." (1 Samuel 16.7) Young David was not the obvious candidate to succeed Saul but he was God's choice.

Often the Scripture portrays the "all seeing" nature of God as a reason for fear. He who knows not only the outward actions but the inner motives is in a better position to judge and therefore must be feared. In this instance, however, it is not judgement but help that Paul has in mind.

KINDLING QUOTE

"New grief, new hope he will bestow
Thy grief and pain to quell;
Into thy heart himself will go,
And that will make thee well."

Young David was not the obvious candidate...

DAY 32

The struggling, suffering Christian who does not even know how or what to pray has One who knows every circumstance and even the deep emotions of the heart. God knows our breaking point.

He is like the father who had taken his young son shopping. As they wandered around the supermarket the father would put various items into the basket which his son was carrying. Another shopper thought, as she saw the boy carrying what appeared to her to be a heavy basket, that it was too much for the lad. "Isn't that a little bit too heavy for you?" she asked.

"Oh no," said the boy, "my dad knows just how much I can carry."

The Holy Spirit knows how much we can bear because He sees in the deep hidden recesses of the believer's heart and mind. He knows, too, how to draw the best out of us so that we keep going - onward and upward.

Not only does the Holy Spirit know us, if indeed He lives in us, He also makes known to us the heart and mind of our Father God. This is a breathtaking truth. "No eye has seen, no ear has heard, no mind has conceived, what God has prepared for those who love him - but God has revealed it to us by his Spirit. The Spirit searches all things even the deep things of God." (1 Corinthians 2.9-10) Wow!!

I know you really want to read 1 Corinthians 2, but sorry, I want you to read his second letter to the Corinthians 2.6-16, and meditate on verse 10.

FIRESTARTER VERSE

Search me, O God, and know my heart; test me and know my anxious thoughts
(Psalm 139.23)

Because the Spirit intercedes for the saints in accordance with God's will (8.27b)

DAY 33

Have you ever plugged in an electrical appliance which you bought at a bargain price overseas only to have it burn-out the motor because the current was different?

Having done that myself I was ready when an American singing group visited England and needed to use electricity for their keyboards and P.A. system. A friend built me a somewhat hefty transformer to convert from one current to the other.

That is close to what the Holy Spirit does for the believer. If we were to get always what we prayed for no doubt our motors would burn out. We do not always know what is best for us because we cannot see as God sees the full circumstances and implications of our prayers. As Paul has already pointed out, we do not know what to pray for.

The Holy Spirit acts, if I may put it like this, as a transformer. He searches the deep recesses of our hearts and minds and is able to convert what He sees there into an intercession, a prayer, to fit God's will and purpose.

God will never answer a prayer except in accordance with His own purpose. The ever practical James reminds us of this truth. He warns, "You do not receive, because you ask with wrong motives, that you may spend what you get on your pleasures." (James 4.3)

Paul's experience is a good lesson. In addition to his many hardships he is given, he says, "a thorn in the flesh". We may only guess what it was and probably guess wrong; but he goes on to tell how he prayed to God three times, even pleaded with Him to have this thorn removed.

However, it was not taken away. Was it because he lacked faith? Was it because God did not hear? Was God not powerful enough to remove it?

Paul shares with us the answer, because the same Holy Spirit who searched Paul's motives also searched God's will and revealed it. "My grace is sufficient for you, for my power is made perfect in weakness." (2 Corinthians 12.9)

KINDLING QUOTE

"If we will but let our God and Father work his will with us, there can be no limit to his enlargement of our existence, to the flood of life with which he will overflow our consciousness."

DAY 33

Indeed, it does take a special kind of grace to accept that God does not always take away our suffering. That has been the recurring theme in these verses. Groaning always has a cause and the cause is not always removed.

Prayer may be likened to a cheque which needs two signatures. When it is prayed, the cheque is, as it were, sent to heaven for Gods' counter-signature. If it comes back unsigned it may be because God is writing one of His own for you to counter-sign just as He did with Paul.

Accepting God's will is what makes us saints. For a saint is not a separate class of super-Christian but any believer. It means holy or set apart: one who is reserved for God's purpose: one who does God's will.

Read Psalm 139 and ask God the Holy Spirit to search your heart and to enable you to know God's will for today.

FIRESTARTER VERSE

Do not be quick with your mouth, do not be hasty in your heart to utter anything before God. God is in heaven and you are on earth, so let your words be few

(Ecclesiastes 5.2)

And we know that in all things God works together for the good of those who love him (8.28a)

DAY 34

Do you ever feel the same as I do, that when you are just going through one of those grotty moments in life, somebody comes up with a "precious" text. You know the sort of thing I mean - everything seems to be going wrong and somebody says "Never mind. All things work together for good."

I want to scream, not just because they are trivialising the harsh realities of life, but because they have taken a strong text and wrenched it out of its Biblical context.

At best it is reduced to a romantic, pseudo-spiritual notion of wishful thinking, unless it is grounded in what Paul has already said about the Holy Spirit interceding for the saints *apropos* God's will.

There is, therefore, a qualification. The Scripture is not saying that God works everything to the good of all. That is patently not so. Not all are "saints". Not all love Him. There is, however, even for the believer a further qualification.

Paul is not saying there will be freedom from pain and suffering. He has already made plain that suffering is part and parcel of our common humanity and creatureliness. The rain falls on the just and the unjust. The believer suffers even more because of his battle with inner sin and the possibility of persecution.

Neither is he saying, to those who are in the thick of suffering, a spiritualized version of "It'll all come out in the wash!" It may not, in the sense of personal comfort. The promise may be neither profitable nor advantageous in the short term nor even the long term. That is not to deny that God does bless His children. Thankfully, His grace and mercy does extend to His loved ones here and now. He delights to give. But that is not what Paul is saying in this particular verse.

What then, I hear you ask, is he saying? The key is in the context. Paul has, throughout the whole chapter, focussed his readers' attention on the confident hope of full salvation even in the face of trials and death. The path to glory must necessarily go through the valley of trials and temptations but for those who love Him and are dedicated to fulfilling His purposes, God will ultimately bring every circumstance together for good. That is the fulfilment of all His salvation promises of eternal life.

KINDLING QUOTE

"The true child, the righteous man, will trust absolutely, against all appearances, the God who has created in him the love of righteousness."

DAY 34

The apostle no doubt had in mind the former covenant with Israel in which love and obedience toward God were the national response to His deliverance from slavery in Egypt. They were to maintain love and faithfulness as God, their national saviour, took them through the trials of the wilderness toward the promised land, the land flowing with milk and honey, the land of God's goodness. Read about this in Deuteronomy 11.1-15.

There is, therefore, nothing glib about this saying. God may contrive to bring, out of even the worst circumstances, our temporal good. But on the other hand, He may not. The blind christian may still need a guide dog! God will, however, use everything, good and bad, to bring His sons and daughters into their good inheritance.

As Paul put it earlier, "since we have been justified through faith, we have peace with God through our Lord Jesus Christ, through whom we have gained access by faith into this grace in which we now stand."

And we rejoice in the hope of the glory of God. Not only so, but we also rejoice in our sufferings" (Romans 5.1-3).

FIRESTARTER VERSE

Though he slay me, yet will I hope in him
(Job 13.15)

Those who love him (8.28b)

DAY 35

One night as I was putting my then four year old daughter to bed she put her arms around my neck and said, "Daddy, I love you."

"Oh," said I teasingly. "How much do you love me?"

"This much," she replied, flinging her arms as wide as she could stretch them. "How much do you love me?" she quizzed with a twinkle of expectancy.

"Infinitely," I responded, throwing my arms wider than hers.

"What's infinitely?" she said with a furrow to her tiny brow.

"Oh that means the biggest kind of love. It's higher than the stars in the sky. It's deeper than the deepest ocean. It never comes to an end." I looked to see if she understood. She smiled comfortably and seemed about to settle down to sleep when suddenly her eyes danced and sparkled and she threw her arms around me once more.

"Daddy," she said in mock accusation, "you can't love me infinitely. Only God can love like that."

Thereafter, till this day if ever I ask Christy how much she loves me the answer is invariably, "Infinitely - minus one." The lesson has never been lost. "God is love." (1 John 4.8) When He loves He does so because it is His very nature to love.

But, as C. S. Lewis once said, "On the whole, God's love for us is a much safer subject to think about than our love for him."

In truth, our love is a wisp, a passing shadow, compared to His great love but none the less essential to God's plan. For without our love toward God, His would be infinite but isolated. Without reciprocation there is no relationship. And it is relationship that is in God's heart.

As Paul said, "the man who loves God is known by God." (1 Corinthians 8.3) That knowledge is not a distant indifference but a warm intimate relationship and part of God's ultimate purpose.

KINDLING QUOTE

"In every burning heart, in everything that hopes and fears and is, love is the creative presence, the centre, the source of life - yea life itself; yea God himself."

DAY 35

Our love for God can only be in the spirit, because the "sinful mind", as we saw earlier, is "hostile to God". Hence Paul's assertion that "God has poured out his love into our hearts by the Holy Spirit, whom he has given us." (Romans 5.5) He loved us so much that He even gave to us the ability to love Him, and to respond to His love. This may be why the New Testament says so very little about our love for God. For even though it may grow and become an "undying love" its origin is in God's love for us.

As John says, "This is love: not that we loved God, but that he loved us and sent his Son as an atoning sacrifice for our sins." (1 John 4.10)

As you read 1 John 4.7-21 meditate on the way in which God's love, having been extended to you, is to flow not only back to Him but also outward to your brothers and sisters in the household of faith.

FIRESTARTER VERSE

No eye has seen, no ear has heard, no mind has conceived what God has prepared for those who love him (I Corinthians 2.9)

Who have been called according to his purpose (8.28c) — DAY 36

It seems that we human beings are by nature clannish. We have a natural bias toward tribalism as though our security is in belonging to some entity larger than ourselves. At its best this inclination leads to the solidarity of patriotism and what the French so eloquently call *esprit de corps*. At its worst it is liable to degenerate into chauvinistic bigotry, prejudice, hatred and war.

Even within that body of people called out of every nation to be the people of God, among whom there are to be no such divisions as race, colour, gender or social status differences emerge. Unless we are careful all too soon we are duped into abandoning the ideal of unity in Christ for the murky waters of supposed theological purity.

I am so glad that Peter found his fellow apostle's writings "hard to understand". But what a pity that succeeding generations did not heed his warning that, "ignorant and unstable people distort ..." (2 Peter 3.16) what they do not understand. Instead of walking in humility in a common search after truth we all too easily split into camps and factions all of which are by definition right. Calvinists and Arminians, charismatics and non-charismatics, Episcopal and Congregational, conservative and liberal, high church, low church, no church, two toad in the hole, double chips and peas!

There is danger that whenever we come to certain of these "hard sayings" that we don our theologically-tinted glasses and see them from partisan preconceptions instead of praying for the Holy Spirit to illuminate His word.

Let us then tread gently together these verses which have divided Christians for centuries. Even if we are unable to settle the dispute over "call" and "election" let us learn the better lesson that our belonging to Christ and the family of God is not dependent upon answering all the questions but on God's unqualified grace to sinful men and women.

Paul is not here concerned with the nature of God's call. He is writing as an apostle commissioned by God to preach the gospel to the non-Jewish world. He is to assure them that what the people of Israel presumed to be a covenant with their nation alone is a call to all, including Gentiles. (Romans 1.5)

KINDLING QUOTE

"How terribly have theologians misrepresented God's character. The simplest peasant who loves his children and his sheep would be the true type of our God beside that monstrosity of a monarch."

DAY 36

As a Jew himself he is delighted to say to the young church in Rome "you also are among those who are called to belong to Jesus Christ. .... who are loved by God and called to be saints." (Romans 1.6-7) Now he reminds them again that their confident hope is in a God who works everything for the good of those who love Him and are called according to His purpose. And what is His purpose? That the Gentiles should be called "My people" (Romans 9.24-25) and receive an inheritance.

Far from being limited, the call is extended outwards from the Jews to "everyone who calls on the name of the Lord" (Romans 10:13).

Does this mean that God changed His mind about Israel? No! Ten thousand times no! The following chapters 9-11 have much to say about Israel receiving an inheritance. Read chapter 10 for yourself - and remember, walk humbly.

... found his fellow apostle's writings "hard to understand", as we do today.

FIRESTARTER VERSE

God has called us to live in peace (I Corinthians 7.15b)

For those God foreknew he also predestined (8.29a)

DAY 37

I was recently the guest preacher at the opening of a new church in Stubbington where the minister's vestry has a window that looks out to the entrance foyer. From inside the vestry, with the light off, I could see who was coming to church. They, however, could not see me because from the foyer the window appeared to be a mirror. Therefore, I saw the congregation long before they saw me. I knew beforehand who was coming to church. To this extent I had a certain amount of foreknowledge.

In a much more magnificent way God had foreknowledge from within eternity concerning who would respond to His call to believe in Jesus as Lord and Saviour. He foreknew those who would be justified by faith and those who would not. There is nothing in the word "foreknew" to indicate that God was pro-active in determining who should and who should not believe any more than my seeing the congregation arrive at church was more than mere observation.

Clearly the word "foreknew" is not equivalent to chose, elected or any such predetermined act. To say it is, is not only reading more into the text than is already there, it actually violates the progressive nature of the sentence. It would be like saying, "Those whom God predestined he also predestined."

That said, the foreknowledge is not so open-ended that it includes everyone. God obviously foreknew every person who ever lived or will live. That does not mean that all are predestined to share in what God has planned for those who love Him, any more than my sermon, which was prepared for anyone who would like to hear it, could have any benefit for those who did not respond to the invitation to attend Stubbington Baptist Church.

On the other hand, knowledge of a person within its biblical context does have the connotation of love. When, for instance, Jesus said in His prayer, "this is eternal life: that they may **know** you, the only true God, and Jesus Christ, whom you have sent" (John 17.3), it was more than head knowledge. It carried with it the idea once made popular in a song title - "To know, know, know him is to love, love, love him." This is why He said to the false followers, "I never knew you." (Matthew 7.23)

KINDLING QUOTE

"Might that is not born of love is not might born from above."

DAY 37

The other side of that coin is that the true followers are like sheep who know the voice of the Good Shepherd who said, "I know my sheep and my sheep know me - just as the Father knows me and I know the Father - and I lay down my life for the sheep." (John 10:14-15)

Knowing and loving come together in the relationship whether it is between God and His only begotten Son or the Good Shepherd and His sheep.

Read John 10:1-18.

FIRESTARTER VERSE

God's solid foundation stands firm, sealed with this inscription: "the Lord knows those who are His"
(2 Timothy 2.19)

To be conformed to the likeness of his Son (8.29)

DAY 38

God's foreknowledge could see what most throughout the history of Israel were incapable of seeing, even though it had always been the bottom-line of the covenant relationship. Namely, that the Gentiles would at last be drawn into the covenant by Christ. God has said to Abraham, "all nations of the earth will be blessed because you have obeyed me." (Genesis 22.18)

The whole point of predestination is lost if the focus is on who is and who is not to be saved because it is not a matter of exclusion but inclusion. The Jews are God's people chosen by grace who, against all the evidence of history, God has predestined to glory (Romans 9-11). But now Paul seals the confidence of the Gentile believers in Rome by showing that God foreknew in eternity past that they, too, would love Him. They, like the Jews, are part of God's family planning, to bring out of every nation an eternal family. In other words, the Gentiles are as elect as the Jews (see Ephesians 2). Through Jesus we all have access to the Father by one Spirit. We Gentiles are excluded no longer but become "faith brothers" - members of God's household (Ephesians 2.18-19).

We are, Jew and Gentile alike, predestined to be like our elder "Divine Brother", Jesus, who Himself was the very image of God. (Colossians 1.15) In other words we are to take on the family likeness. An adopted child, as I know full well, needs to know the ways of the new family. The best way is to see how other children in the family relate to the parents and vice-versa.

It is not without significance that whenever the matter of election is mentioned in the New Testament it is always in the context of Christian behaviour. Our calling is not just to receive God's grace, justification, atonement (at-one-ment), wonderful though these truths are. We are reconciled to God to be His children and are to behave as such - like Jesus. In fact our behaviour is the test by which we know we have become the children of God. (2 Peter 1.10-11)

KINDLING QUOTE

"The salvation of Christ, is salvation from the smallest tendency or leaning to sin. It is salvation that makes the heart pure, with the will and choice of the heart to be pure."

DAY 38

We are to become like Jesus. The word used here for "likeness" is in the Greek, *eikon*. We get from it our English word icon which means a representation or portrait. In the Greek-Roman world, however, it had a legal meaning. In those days, long before the custom of signing one's name became the means of identifying a person's agreement to a document, a description of the person was listed. This list was called an *eikon* because it fully described the person, so that if at a later stage you wished to check who had made the contract, you would simply tick off each item of the *eikon*. We are to become like God's first-born, His only begotten Son, who by His death and resurrection has brought from among both Jews and Gentiles the family which God had planned for Himself.

As you read Colossians 3.1-17 make a list of all the moral defects which belong to the old *eikon* and surrender them to God. Then list all the virtues of "God's chosen people" and see what you must do in verse 10.

FIRESTARTER VERSE

And we, who with unveiled faces all reflect the Lord's glory, are being transformed into his likeness with ever-increasing glory, which comes from the Lord who is the Spirit
(2 Corinthian 3.18)

That he might be the first-born among many brothers (8.29b)

DAY 39

Yesterday, we noted that stage one in God's audacious plan, which He foreordained for those who love Him, is played out in the arena of this life. Controlled by the Spirit (v.8) we are to "put to death the misdeeds of the body" (v.13) and become new by being "conformed" to the very likeness of Jesus. The change involves suffering (v.18) as we take off the old nature and put on a new "Christ-like" self (Colossians 3.9-10).

We are not able alone to reach this standard of holiness (sainthood v.27) so He who came to identify with fallen humanity as God's first-born helps us in our weakness (v.26).

Jesus is not "unable to sympathize with our weaknesses" because He was "tempted in every way, just as we are - yet was without sin" (Hebrews 4.15). So, "because he himself suffered when he was tempted, he is able (by His Spirit) to help those who are being tempted." (Hebrews 2.18)

The second stage of God's plan is resurrection. This is undoubtedly what Paul has in mind here when he uses the term first-born. Jesus was the first-born by way of status as the only begotten of the Father. He is called "the first-born over all creation" (Colossians 1.15) as part of His own identity, as the "*eikon*-image" of God. But He was also "the beginning and the first-born from among the dead." (Colossians 1.18)

As we have already observed, the resurrection, (that is our own resurrection), is at the end of what I have called the "between-times", the gap between responding in humble submission to the gospel and death. Only then is the continuing act of salvation completed. The heirs of God and co-heirs with Christ enter into the inheritance which was planned before the foundation of the earth.

The adopted sons and daughters enter the place prepared for them by their elder Divine Brother, who promised, "if I go to prepare a place for you, I will come back and take you to be with me that you also may be where I am." (John 14.2-3)

KINDLING QUOTE

"'Eternal Brother,' we cry, 'Show us the Father. Be thyself to us, that in thee we may know him. We too are his children. Let the other children share with thee in the things of the Father.'"

DAY 39

No wonder the apostle almost explodes with praise as he writes to the church at Ephesus, "Praise be to the God and Father our Lord Jesus Christ, who has blessed us in the heavenly realms with every spiritual blessing in Christ. For he chose us in him before the creation of the world to be holy and blameless in his sight. In love he predestined us to be adopted as his sons through Jesus Christ...". (Ephesians 1.3-5)

We who love Him and are called according to His purpose are able then to see that His purpose was firstly for this life, that we should be like His Son by becoming holy. Secondly, that we should become one of the "many brothers" - and sisters - who in turn enter God's eternal home. Christ the first-born, followed by the first-fruits, that is those who have already died (1 Corinthians 15.20,23) and last of all those who are still alive at His coming again. (1 Thessalonians 4.17)

As you read Hebrews chapter 2 make a list of all the things Jesus, your Eternal Elder Brother, has done for you.

FIRESTARTER VERSE

And just as we have borne the likeness of the earthly man, so shall we bear the likeness of the man from heaven (1 Corinthians 15.49)

And those he predestined, he also called (8.30a)

DAY 40

Art Linkletter saw a small boy drawing a picture and inquired of him, "What's that you are drawing?"

"Oh, it's just a picture of God," replied the boy.

Art Linkletter, seeing the opportunity to educate the lad in spiritual matters told him, "No-one knows what God looks like."

The boy thought about this for a moment and returned to his drawing, and confidently said, "Well, they will when I've finished this."

I am conscious that many finer minds than mine have grappled with this text to portray a true picture of God. I have often felt that my feeble efforts to understand the Scripture are like night-time photography without a flash-gun. At best the image is blurred.

However, the path to God and His truth has been worn by feet of little children with inquisitive minds. If you will be a child with me we shall walk together. If you insist on your doctrine because greater men have formed it, I shall tell you that children care little for doctrine but much for the Father.

KINDLING QUOTE

"Had the wise and prudent been the confidants of God the letter would have usurped the place of the Spirit and a system of religion, with its rickety malodorous plan of salvation, would have been put in the place of a living Christ."

87

DAY 40

My understanding to date leads me to this conclusion, which I launch in good faith, not as doctrine but as a child on a paper-chase might say, "Here's a clue. Can this be its meaning?"

Paul, a Jew, was no doubt surprised when God called him to be an apostle to the Gentiles (Acts 26.17). Now as he writes to the Gentile church in Rome he makes clear that he has this upper-most in his mind. "We received grace and apostleship to call people from among all the Gentiles to the obedience that comes from faith. And you also are among those who are called to belong to Jesus Christ .... called to be saints." (Romans 1.5-7)

From our 20th century vantage point we cannot begin to appreciate what this meant. The Jews were the chosen people. They were the predestined. They were the called. They were the children of promise, not the Gentiles.

For the first five chapters Paul shows how the fore-ordained plan of God is a gospel of salvation for both Jew and Gentile. All would be justified by faith and reconciled to God and brought to eternal life. For the next three chapters he answers the question posed in 6.1, "Shall we go on sinning so that grace may increase?" But from the beginning of chapter eight he has been assuring his Gentile friends that there is no condemnation for those who are in Christ. They are to be confident of their adoption into God's plan which far from being an after-thought was predestined or, to use an equally acceptable word, fore-ordained.

This verse then has nothing to do with whether one person is damned because he was not predestined to salvation. Hence Paul's confident assertion "There is no difference between Jew and Gentile - the same Lord is Lord of all and richly blesses all who call on him, for, 'Everyone who calls on the name of the Lord will be saved.'" (Romans 10:12-13)

The elect are God's people, the church.

God will confirm this truth to your heart as you read Ephesians 2.

FIRESTARTER VERSE

In love he predestined us to be adopted as his sons through Jesus Christ, in accordance with his pleasure and will (Ephesians l.5)

Those he called, he also justified; those he justified, he also glorified (8.30b)

DAY 41

Suppose I were a homeless squatter and I were to break into your house, but as I climb through your window I am seen by one of your neighbours, who immediately calls the police. The house is surrounded. I am caught red-handed.

A few weeks later I am in the dock listening to the evidence against me. My guilt is obvious to all. The judge says, "Mr. Jackopson, have you anything to say in your defence?"

"I have not."

"Do you have anything you wish to tell the court?" he asks.

"Yes I do sir," I reply. "I'm sorry about what I did and promise I'll never do it again."

"Oh," says the judge, "but I am here to dispense justice. Therefore, I shall fine you £500.00."

"But judge," I complain, "I have no money and no job."

Imagine this. The judge goes to the clerk of the court, takes out his own cheque book and writes a cheque for £500.00. Do you see what he has done? The just penalty which he imposed has been paid in full and at the same time I have been freed from the penalty because of the judge's mercy.

As I walk out of the court the judge says to me, "Now keep your nose clean. No more house-breaking, d'ya hear?"

I promise him I shall "go straight".

Fanciful? Yes, it may be. But that is quite close to what God did for His children. Jesus, the judge, (John 5.27) has paid the penalty for our sins as an atoning sacrifice. This is how John puts it, "This is love: not that we loved God, but that he loved us and sent his Son as an atoning sacrifice for our sins." (1 John 4.10)

KINDLING QUOTE

"Jesus sacrificed himself to his Father and the children to bring them together - all the love on the side of the Father and the Son, all the selfishness on the side of the children."

DAY 41

Paul put it in even more judicial terms, "This righteousness from God comes through faith in Jesus Christ to all who believe. There is no difference, for all have sinned and fall short of the glory of God, and are justified freely by his grace through the redemption that came by Christ Jesus."

God presented him as a sacrifice of atonement, through faith in his blood." Read this in context in Romans chapter 3. You will find my little story helpful as you understand the two sides of God's character - His love and His justice.

If your confidence and faith is in Him you may say that you are justified (just-as-if-I'd-never sinned) and living in the promise of being glorified; at home with Him and His Son, your Brother and Saviour.

FIRESTARTER VERSE

And God raised us up with Christ and seated us with him in the heavenly realms in Christ Jesus (Ephesians 2.6)

What, then, shall we say in response to this? If God is for us, who can be against us? (8.31)

DAY 42

C. H. Spurgeon tells a story of a man who was invited by a friend to taste an apple in his orchard. "I'd rather not," said the visitor, "I've tasted your apples and they are sour."

"Oh!" said his friend. "When did you taste my apples?"

"When I was a boy I used to pick up the wind-falls that fell the other side of the fence."

"Ah, yes," chuckled the owner, "they are as sour as old crab-apples. My father planted them there to fool would be "scrumpers". When you get into the orchard the rest of the fruit is delicious."

Spurgeon then makes this point. "Around the border of religion, along the outer hedge, there are some sour apples, of conviction, self-denial, humiliation and self-despair, planted on purpose to keep off hypocrites and mere professors; but in the midst of the garden are luscious fruits, mellow to the taste, and sweet as nectar. The central position in religion is the sweetest. The nearer to God the sweeter the joy."

The whole question about predestination has been for many "sour apples". Some have been dissuaded from entering the orchard because its heartiest exponents have appeared to be harsh, uncompromising bigots, more interested in maintaining their doctrinal positions than encouraging others to come taste and see that the Lord is good.

Not so the apostle, as he makes this link between the "no condemnation" of the first verse and "no separation" in the last. He says in effect: God is on your side. He who was on the side of Israel, has now shown His hand. The mystery, which had been "kept hidden for ages and generations", was now out in the open (Colossians 1.26). And what was that mystery? Glorious good news for all! "That through the gospel the Gentiles are heirs together with Israel, members together of one body, and sharers together in the promise in Christ Jesus." (Ephesians 3.6) The chosen people are no longer a single nation but brethren from every nation under the sun. The God who appeared for a while to be exclusively on the side of Israel is "for us"; that is, for all who love him and cry "Abba, Father".

KINDLING QUOTE

"The devotion of God to his creatures is perfect."

DAY 42

If God had planned all of this from eternity past to be concluded in eternity future then the glory to come - the inheritance - is secure, "stored up for you in heaven" (Colossians 1.5). What happens in "the between-times" is of little consequence. Paul is not saying there will be no struggles, no battles, no enemies. He is saying no matter what life throws in your path, no matter who stands against you - the might of the state, the power of commerce, enemies religious or secular - they are all of them insignificant alongside the God who rules from eternity through time to eternity. As Pascal once put it, "The greatest single distinguishing feature of the omnipotence of God is that our imagination gets lost when thinking about it."

Read the twenty-third Psalm with confident hope in the God who is on your side.

FIRESTARTER VERSE

He will cover you with his feathers, and under his wings you will find refuge; his faithfulness will be your shield and rampart (Psalm 91.4)

He who did not spare his own Son, but gave him up for us all - how will he not also, along with him, graciously give us all things? (8.32)

DAY 43

A railway worker had charge of a drawbridge over the Mississippi. A large ship had just gone under the up-raised bridge when he heard the 1.00 p.m. Memphis train sounding its whistle to warn of its speedy approach. The attendant was unconcerned. The bridge was already on its way down. Suddenly, however, he heard a scream. His small son, who had come in to spend time talking to his father, had wandered off to watch the ship passing beneath him. He had lost his footing and fallen into the huge gears.

The father was faced with an awful choice. If he stopped the bridge lowering he might save his son. But if he did this the 1.00 p.m. Memphis express would plunge into the Mississippi with the loss of many lives. As the train roared over the bridge the grief-stricken father could see passengers reading their papers, drinking their coffee, sleeping. In despair the man shouted, "Don't you care. I sacrificed my son for you." Some waved back at him. Then all was quiet.

This true story is touching, and no-one would minimise the sacrifice of that desperate father, but God's sacrifice was even greater. It was no accident. He "did not spare his own Son, but gave him up". It was a willing sacrifice. God presented Him as a sacrifice of atonement (3.25). "He was delivered over to death for our sins" (4.25) as a demonstration of God's love for us (5.8).

Was Jesus the unwilling victim in all this? There is never a note of reproach from Him. As He said to Nicodemus, "God so loved the world that he gave his one and only Son, that whoever believes in him shall not perish but have eternal life." (John 3.16) To his enemies he said, "I lay down my life for the sheep. .... The reason my Father loves me is that I lay down my life." (John 10:15,17)

It is possible that Paul had in mind here, the irony of how the nation of the Jews was born out of the willingness of Abraham to sacrifice his son Isaac, which God would not allow him to do. Yet God Himself not only wills it but does it for His blood bought family by giving His only, unadopted Son for us "all", both Jew and Gentile.

KINDLING QUOTE

"God is the origin of both need and supply, the Father of our necessities, the abundant giver of all good things. Gloriously he meets the claims of his child."

DAY 43

The "giving up" of His Son is now expanded and reinforced by a further act of grace as He "graciously gives us all things" along with everything He has given to His only true Son and heir.

Sons and daughters who are used to the sacrificial giving of their parents have no doubts about the durability of their generosity. Neither need we doubt that having sacrificed so much for our salvation, God will be anything other than faithful to all His promises - those for this life and equally, those in the life to come in glory.

Read Isaiah 53 and see whether God can be trusted.

FIRESTARTER VERSE

**From the fullness of his grace we have all received one blessing after another
(John 1.16)**

Who will bring any charge against those whom God has chosen? It is God who justifies (8.33)

DAY 44

Paul, loyal to the theme now well established that all who put their faith in Christ are heirs to the covenant, deliberately, it seems to me, bestows on the believer the Jewish title "chosen" - elect. Moses had said to the wandering Israelites during the "inbetween-time" of liberation from Egypt and entering the promised land, "The Lord your God has chosen you out of all the peoples on the face of the earth to be his people, his treasured possession." (Deuteronomy 7.6) They were called "sons of Jacob, his chosen ones." (Psalm 105.6) But now, in the new "inbetween-times", the resurrection-to-glory gap, it is the adopted children of God who are called "chosen".

We know that the apostle almost lived in the Old Testament book of the prophet of Isaiah. Who can doubt that he had Isaiah 50:8-9 on his mind when he penned the words of our text. Listen to what was said. "He who vindicates me is near. Who then will bring charges against me? .... Who is my accuser? Let him confront me! It is the Sovereign Lord who helps me. Who is he that will condemn me?"

God fulfilled the prophetic word in Christ. There can be no serious accusation on the last day. If God Himself has already been satisfied that Christ paid the penalty for our sins, then not even Satan, that "accuser of the brethren" (Revelation 12.10) will have anything to say.

We are like those Brazilian Panchos who, seeing a prairie fire coming, "back burn" the grass surrounding them. When the prairie fire sweeps past them they are on ground already burned. Christ made the ground of judgement safe.

Satan cannot accuse. Neither can the law. Neither can they who point the finger at our feeble efforts at being Christlike. Neither can our conscience. It may have once (Romans 2.15) but now it is like a lion, caged. It lives, it may even roar, but because of the bars it cannot molest.

KINDLING QUOTE

"Think brothers, think sisters, we walk in the air of an eternal and loving and forgiving fatherhood."

DAY 44

FIRESTARTER VERSE

Therefore, since we have been justified through faith, we have peace with God through our Lord Jesus Christ, through whom we have gained access by faith into this grace in which we now stand. And we rejoice in the hope of the glory of God (Romans 5.1)

It is interesting, in the light of his earlier statement, "those whom he called he justified", that here Paul uses the present tense. Perhaps he is concerned that we should have no anxiety as we contemplate the judgement to come. We are justified, and are daily being justified, to the end. Self-accusation can be a depressing and draining drag on what ought to be a life of joy and peace. This bold assertion, coming in the afterglow of his earlier triumphal affirmation, "If God is for us, who can be against us?" is quite deliberate. It demands the answer, no one; no thing; no sin.

But, someone will answer, does this mean I may go back to my old habits? No! It means that daily we must come back to Him who justifies and stand on that "burned ground".

Listen to what Paul says elsewhere. "Once you were alienated from God and were enemies in your minds because of your evil behaviour. But now he has reconciled you by Christ's physical body through death to present you holy in his sight, without blemish and free from accusation - if you continue in your faith, established and firm, not moved from the hope held out in the gospel." (Colossians 1.21-23)

Go back now to Romans 2 to see what God has to say about judging others.

Who is he that condemns? Christ Jesus, who died - more than that, who was raised to life - is at the right hand of God and is also interceding for us (8.34)

DAY 45

The earliest creed of the Christian church made four great affirmations about Jesus Christ. He died, He was raised from the dead, He ascended into heaven to sit at the right hand of the Father, and it is He who will judge all at the appointed time.

We have three of the four here - at least. Each is to drive a nail into the coffin of condemnation as a final enactment of Paul's opening declaration of "no condemnation" for those who are in Christ Jesus.

Who is it then that condemns? Not Satan. He is defeated, and at the judgement his accusations hold no weight.

It certainly is not Christ Jesus, for the very purpose for which he came was himself to pay the penalty for the sins of all who believe. He would not undermine his own work of salvation.

It is not only by His death that we are saved. That would be only half the story. It is by His death and resurrection that we live. To the church at Ephesus Paul wrote, "God, who is rich in mercy, made us alive with Christ even when we were dead in transgressions - it is by grace you have been saved. And God raised us up with Christ and seated us with him in the heavenly realms in Christ Jesus." (Ephesians 2.5-6)

I do not want to stretch this point further than Paul intended, but it does appear that the apostle believed so strongly in the effectiveness and completion of Christ's saving work, that our own resurrection is a *fait accompli*. We are co-raised and in some mysterious way already "hidden with Christ in God" (Colossians 3.3), "seated in the heavenly realms".

Christ Himself is seated at the right hand of God. In biblical symbolism, the right hand was a place of power. In the hymn of Moses the Israelites sang "Your right hand, O Lord, was majestic in power. Your right hand, O Lord, shattered the enemy." (Exodus 15.6) But it was without a doubt the prophecy of Psalm 110:1 which gave rise to the early church view of Christ in glory, seated at God's right hand as vice-Regent. Even as early as Pentecost Peter refers to Him as "exalted to the right hand of God." (Acts 2.33)

KINDLING QUOTE

"To the same homeness which Jesus felt in his Father's world, I think all we humans are destined to rise."

DAY 45

The picture is magnificent. The obedient Son waiting, "the one whom God appointed as judge", (Acts 10:42) to receive His adopted brothers and sisters. He is seated (Colossians 3.1) because His work is finished. And there at the throne the Son and the Father converse. What are they saying?

We may only guess. But this much we know, Jesus Christ, Eternal Priest, "is able to save completely those who come to God through him, because he always lives to intercede for them." (Hebrews 7.25) Not enough? Then try Jesus Christ the Righteous One our Eternal Advocate who, "speaks to the Father in our defence" (1 John 2.1). Who is he that condemns?" Silence!

Now read 1 Corinthians 15.1-28. It is all about resurrection!

FIRESTARTER VERSE

For he bore the sin of many, and made intercession for the transgressors (Isaiah 53.12c)

Who shall separate us from the love of Christ? Shall trouble or hardship or persecution or famine or nakedness or danger or sword? (8.35)

DAY 46

Three thousand converts to Christ and all of them baptised in a mass baptism in a single day. Pentecost! It must have seemed to those first apostles that nothing could stand in the way of this people movement. Repentance, forgiveness and the gift of the Holy Spirit must have seemed an unbeatable triad in bringing people to salvation in a risen and exalted Lord. Oozing confidence it bursts forth onto the stage of religious history as the church of Jesus Christ is born.

The cross must have seemed like the fading memory of birth pangs, receding daily into the mists of a half forgotten dream. Joy had come with the morning that first day of the week fifty days ago. Now all was glory and excitement, "praising God and enjoying the favour of all the people. And the Lord added to their number daily those who were being saved." (Acts 2.47)

Then, bang - the prison door slams on Peter and John (Acts 5.18). More arrests. Hastily convened religious courts. Then Stephen. A pile of blood-stained rocks, the temporary tomb stones of the first in a succession of martyrs (Acts 7). Wham! the persecution came as an avalanche scattering the church throughout the Mediterranean world (Acts 8.1).

What had gone wrong? Had God deserted them? Had not Jesus promised power and His own living presence to the very end of the age?

Soon the memory of the cross and the warning words of its victim, would jolt their triumphalism as the realization of suffering and death crowded their senses. One can almost hear the apostles telling their naive disciples about the Master's instructions on what to do when brought before accusers (Luke 12.11,12).

Three thousand ... baptised ... in a single day.

KINDLING QUOTE

"Lay the loved hand upon my head,
Let thy heart beat in mine;
One thought from thee, when all seems dead,
Will make the darkness shine."

DAY 46

Paul was himself well versed in the coinage of persecution: indeed he was a veritable connoisseur. He had been the prime mover, savagely assaulting the saints, only to have the tables turned bringing upon his own head the full wrath of God's enemies. Why, in one list of his own experiences all and more than this list of trouble, hardship, persecution, famine, nakedness, and danger are mentioned. The only one that is not is the sword, and that only because it had not yet happened. Surely, none were more qualified than he to make this bold assertion, that he who cannot bring condemnation upon the believer, cannot one whit reduce the love of Christ for His own.

Note that it is the love of Christ, not our love for Him. Our affection may rise and fall. Circumstances do sometimes have a bearing upon our love, our loyalty, our devotion. We could even (God forbid) apostacise and wrench our lives away from God, returning to unbelief. That is a sad and damnable choice. (Hebrews 6.4-6) But though, as it were, we might knowingly jump out of His hand, nothing else shall snatch us out of it. (John10:28)

Read 2 Timothy 1.1-12 and meditate on verse 12.

FIRESTARTER VERSE

Blessed are you when people insult you, persecute you and falsely say all kinds of evil against you because of me (Matthew 5.II)

For your sake we face death all day long; we are considered as sheep to be slaughtered (8.36)

DAY 47

He was a Hebrew of Hebrews, one of the twice chosen of God. Ever conscious of his Jewish roots he falls back on a verse from the Psalms (44.22) to draw upon the common heritage of suffering. The picture is profound in its rustic simplicity. We are, he says, like sheep already consigned for slaughter, shambling along to the abattoir.

The Rabbis of his day pointed back to this same verse in lament of their humiliation at the hands of Antiochus who would have the Jews sacrifice to idols at the town of Modin. Mattathias led a rebellion against this order, and escaped with an army of patriots to the desert. But they were pursued and routed. Because they refused to fight on the Sabbath, about one thousand were put to death.

Mattathias escaped and later led a successful rebellion. On his death-bed he said to his sons, "Your bodies are mortal, and subject to fate; but they receive a sort of immortality, by the remembrance of what actions they have done; and I would have you so in love with this immortality, that you may pursue after glory, and that, when you have under-gone the greatest difficulties, you may not scruple, for such things, to lose your lives." [1]

Many, through the ages of human conflict have not scrupled to lose their lives for honour, patriotism and its "sort of immortality". Paul, in effect says shall we do less than be ready to have a share in suffering, when our prize is the everlasting love of Him who sustains us?

I remember as a raw recruit in the army being told, "The time between 23.59 and midnight is your own time - the rest belongs to the army." All the day long, every day, every moment, the believer is on standby ready to face whatever battle may come under the orders of Him who said, "If anyone would come after me, he must deny himself and take up his cross and follow me. For whoever wants to save his life will lose it, but whoever loses his life for me will find it." (Matthew 16.24-26)

KINDLING QUOTE

"Better a death when work is done
Than earth's most favoured birth;
Better a child in God's great house
Than the king of all the earth."

---

[1] William Whiston, *The Works of Josephus* (Hendrickson Publishers) 1987

DAY 47

It is in a way as though we were already dead but moving toward life. There is no bleating in Paul's testimony. "I want to know Christ," he says, "and the power of his resurrection and the fellowship of sharing in his sufferings, becoming like him in his death, and so, somehow, to attain to the resurrection from the dead." (Philippians 3.10)

There is a toughness in his stance which seems strangely alien to modern westernised Christianity where respectability, balance, tolerance and above all, blessing are articles of faith. We rejoice to be part of the flock. Who would not with such a good Shepherd? So long as He leads us beside still waters... so long as He restores our souls... so long as He prepares a table in the presence of our enemies and not an altar or a chopping board... so long as he leads us to pleasant grazing and not through the valley of death... we shall fear no evil. But neither shall we understand the suffering church of other lands; nor how to "rejoice in our sufferings", to develop perseverance, character, and hope (Romans 5.3-5).

Read 2 Corinthians 1.3-11 and see where real comfort comes from.

FIRESTARTER VERSE

We always carry around in our body the death of Jesus, so that the life of Jesus may also be revealed in our body
(2 Corinthians 4.10)

The time between 23.59 and midnight is your own time

No, in all these things we are more than conquerors through him who loved us (8.37)

DAY 48

There is an old Spanish proverb which says "He who would be a Christian must expect crucifixion." Many have been killed because of their faith. More in the last half of the 20th century than in all the preceding centuries. Most of them in Africa and Asia. Whole tribes in North Africa to this very day are starving for no other reason than that they name Jesus as their Lord. It is no longer "by the sword" but the effect is just as final with an AK47 gun. The sheep are still being slaughtered.

Deprivation, loss of homes, unemployment, beatings, starvation, torture and every kind of humiliation are commonplace in our contemporary world. It is almost impossible for the western church to comprehend the human misery some of our brothers and sisters endure as a daily diet of living martyrdom. And yet Paul has the unmitigated audacity to call all these things a triumph. No! More than that! We are more than conquerors in spite of everything. We are excessively victorious - hyper-heroes - ultra-champs. I am not over-stating the case. The Greek word means all of these plus a little bit more.

But how can he be serious? Surely, persecution is a disaster? Yes, it most certainly is for the duration. Some have buckled under its tyranny. Paul is obviously not making light of what he himself had suffered but looking beyond to the prize. As he said to Timothy, toward the end of his life, "I am already being poured out like a drink offering, the time has come for my departure. I have fought the good fight, I have finished the race, I have kept the faith. Now there is in store for me the crown of righteousness." (2 Timothy 4.6-8) He may feel the cold steel of execution but he has no fear of those who can only kill the body but leave the soul intact.

KINDLING QUOTE

"Love is stronger than all force,
Is its own eternal source;
Might is always in decay,
Love grows fresher every day;
Love alone is strength!"

DAY 48

Note how the victory is ours but the facilitator of the conquest is none other than Him who loved us enough to lay down His own life on the cross. Like any good leader, He never asks the troops to do what He would not. There is another sense in which the victory belongs to the persecuted. The testimony of suffering has always touched the hearts of those who witness it. We shall never know the measure to which Paul himself was moved by the death of Stephen the first Christian martyr after Christ. (Acts 7.60) It is surely not without significance that in the Greek language our word "witness" is *martys* - from which we get our English word martyr.

Witnessing has a price-tag. As you read about Paul and Silas' experience of prison in Acts 16.16-33, remember to pray for today's martyr-witnesses.

FIRESTARTER VERSE

Remember those in prison as if you were their fellow prisoners, and those who are mistreated as if you yourselves were suffering (Hebrews 13.3)

I am convinced that neither death nor life, neither angels nor demons, neither the present nor the future, nor any powers, neither height nor depth, nor anything else in all creation, will be able to separate us from the love of God that is in Christ Jesus our Lord (8.38,39)

DAY 49

It is almost thirty-five years since I first read these words and still they make me say, "Wow!" I had just spent three months in Winchester Prison where, through reading a Gideon Bible, I was saved. God had found me in my despair and poured His love into my heart.

Now I was serving a year at Macgregor House Probation Hostel in London's Tulse Hill, and attending Chatsworth Baptist Church. Whether it was a sermon, a Bible study or simply my morning quiet time that brought me face to face with this ending of Romans 8, I have long since forgotten, but I do remember its impact.

"I am convinced"! Eighteen other men around me in that hostel were not - but I was convinced too. In that moment Paul and I became blood-brothers. There was the same inner loathing of sin in my life that had made him testify, "I am unspiritual, sold as a slave to sin. I do not understand what I do. For what I want to do I do not do, but what I hate to do. .... When I want to do good, evil is right there with me. For in my inner being I delight in God's law; but I see another law at work in the members of my body, ... What a wretched man I am! Who will rescue me ....?" (Romans 7.14-15, 21-24)

The biggest surprise in the first weeks of my being a Christian was that the desires were not taken away. Had I not surrendered all? Yet sin lurked in every corner. Had God rejected me as a case too bad for Him? I was desperate to change but a slave to my past and living in a society which was about to burst into the 60's when permissiveness was to be the new order. I was going up the down escalator and often found myself back at the bottom of it.

KINDLING QUOTE

"Doubt must precede every deeper assurance. For uncertainties are what we first see when we look into a region hitherto unknown, unexplored, unannexed."

DAY 49

But I was convinced, and still am, that nothing could then, and nothing shall now, separate me from the love of God because it is the strength of His love that matters. Mine may be weak and vacillating but His love is robust enough to last an eternity. I am convinced!

I have shared my own experience with you because the poetry of these verses is not for dissecting but for accepting. It is fairly obvious that the apostle has penned these words as an all-inclusive list. He says emphatically, nothing, absolutely nothing in the spirit realm or the physical world, no experience now or ever, no powerful attack of the enemy, nothing, absolutely nothing, is going to change God's love toward those who continue to put their faith in Him who justifies.

Today I want you to say with me:

I am convinced, there is no condemnation
I am convinced, there is no separation
I am convinced, I am a child of God
I am not ashamed to believe His word.

Now read the words of Jesus in John 6.35-47 and meditate on verse 47.

FIRESTARTER VERSE

I am not ashamed of the gospel, because it is the power of God for the salvation of every-one who believes: first for the Jew, then for the Gentile (Romans 1.16)

The love of God that is in Christ Jesus our Lord (8.39b)

DAY 50

Before Col. James Irwin, the Apollo 15 astronaut, was promoted to glory, I was privileged to spend many hours listening to his fascinating stories about the 1969 moon landing.

Endeavour had taken him on a voyage of a quarter of a million miles (give or take an inch or two). As they orbited the moon, memories of the Apollo 13 accident must have haunted them. That mission had been aborted because a small explosion had damaged the oxygen and water supply in the lunar module, without which they could not survive on the moon.

At the precisely computed moment, *Falcon* touched down in the Hadley Rille, a huge canyon at the base of a thirteen thousand feet lunar mountain. For three days my friend and Dave Scott explored their surroundings. Jim recalled his verdict, "I can only compare what I see to a desert, but without cactus or any other signs of life." No water, no air, no gravity, no life. The inches of dust would receive their footprints and hold them for a million years.

KINDLING QUOTE

"Our longing desires can no more exhaust the fullness of the treasure of the Godhead, than our imagination can touch their measure."

DAY 50

Without in any way wishing to minimize what by any measurement was an enormous achievement that has given scientists much useful data for further exploration and understanding of our larger habitat, compared to God's mission it was nothing. Jim and Dave could not have survived the inhospitable sphere without wearing their spacesuits to give them an oxygen supply and protection against the scorching 250° Fahrenheit. They met no-one, left no impression save their footprints and a rubbish bag of empty food containers and one used Rover dune-buggy. They brought back samples of rock, one of which, the Genesis Rock, is the oldest to be discovered by man.

Compare that, as I often heard Jim compare it, to God's Earth Mission. He brought no rubbish but returned with what, to Him, was the most precious prize - adopted sons and daughters. "God so loved the world that he gave his one and only Son, that whoever believes in him shall not perish but have eternal life." It was love, love, love, all the way, love.

Our visitor was not an unfeeling Vulcan from the Starship Enterprise. He was the very heart-beat of the one Eternal God who is, in His very nature, Love. He held children in His arms with tenderness. He exposed the hypocrisy of men who would punish an adulterous woman and reassured her that He, the only innocent man, would not condemn her. Such was the power of His leadership that men would abandon their jobs and incomes to follow Him. Such was the gentleness of His Spirit that He could look into the eyes of His friends and say without embarrassment, "As the Father has loved me, so have I loved you." (John 15.9).

Being a Christian is not a matter of just believing right doctrine however important that doctrine might be. God is not a set of theological propositions to be ticked off - He is infinitely personal and is more interested in our love than our correctness. He knows that we get it wrong both in behaviour and belief but He loves us still and longs for our love and loyalty in return.

I pray that you have enjoyed these "Kindlings" and that they will create in you a new fire of confident hope which will spread to others. To God be the glory.

FIRESTARTER VERSE

May the God of hope fill you with all joy and peace as you trust in him, so that you may overflow with hope by the power of the Holy Spirit
(Romans 15.13)

PRAYER OF FAITH

Heavenly Father,
Thank you for loving me.
Thank you for coming in Jesus
to pay the penalty for my sin.
I confess my sin to you now
and ask you to forgive me.
I accept your gift of eternal life.
Help me to live at peace with you
and also with others.
Give me the strength I need
to follow you all the days of my life.
Fill me with your Holy Spirit of love
to love you and to obey you.
In Jesus' name I pray.
Amen

RESURRECTION HYMN

Dying, dying, Christ was dying, To destroy the devil's work.
There upon that gallows buying Our salvation at a stroke.
He our guilt and judgement owning, Proved His love our faithful friend:
God's own sacrifice atoning, So that none need be condemned.

Resting, resting, Christ was resting, In a lonely garden tomb,
Near to where he had been praying, "Father let your will be done."
But the grave could hold no longer, God's own Son, the crucified;
Over death He proved the stronger, That bright day when dark death died.

Risen, risen, Christ has risen, Firstborn from among the dead;
God has raised Him up to heaven, There to reign, exalted head.
Therefore, shall our lungs with gladness, Burst into a cheerful song
Joining voices with the chorus, Of the saints through ages long.

Living, living, Christ is living, Seated in the heavenlies;
Ever loving and forgiving, All our costly penalties.
Children of the resurrection, Whose foundations were of dust
Have received a great salvation, From the Righteous One, the Just.

Coming, coming, Christ is coming, He will come a second time;
Yes, the Mighty One returning, Wrapped in glorious light sublime.
At the trumpet blast relieving, All the dead in Christ will rise
And those who are found believing, Enter into paradise.

© *Vic Jackopson 1993,1994*
May be sung to the tune of Beethoven's "Hymn to Joy"

BIBLIOGRAPHY

Paul's Letter to the Romans, John Ziesler (SCM Press, London, 1990)

Romans - A Shorter Commentary, C.E.B. Cranfield (T & T Clark Ltd., Edinburgh, 1991)

Commentary on St. Paul's Epistle to the Romans, F. Godet, (T & T Clarke Ltd., Edinburgh, 1890)

The Interpretation of St. Paul's Epistle to the Romans, R.C. Lenski, (Augsburg Publishing House, Minneapolis, 1961)

Romans - An Introduction and Commentary, F.F. Bruce, Tyndale Press, London, 1969)

The Epistle of Paul to the Romans, C.H. Dodd, Fontana Books, 1959)

The Interpreter's Bible, Editor Nolan Harmon, (Abingdon Press, Nashville, 1954)

Word Biblical Commentary, James F.G. Dunn, (Word, Incorporated, 1988)

The Epistle to the Romans, Leon Morris, (Wm. B. Eerdmans Publishing Co., 1988)

The Wycliffe Exegetical Commentary, Romans 1-8, Douglas Moo, (Moody Press, Chicago, 1991)

Romans, Joseph A. Fitzmyer, (Geoffrey Chapman, London, 1993)

The Works of Josephus, William Whiston, (Hendrickson Publishers, Massachusetts, 1991)

Destination: Moon, James Irwin, (Multnomah, Oregon, 1989)

Discovering the Character of God, George MacDonald, edited Michael R. Phillips, (Bethany House Publishers, Minneapolis, 1989)

The Solitary Throne, S.M. Zwemer, (Pickering & Inglis, London 1937)

Vic Jackopson has written other books which may be purchased directly from HOPE NOW MINISTRIES.

1978 Evangelism Explosion (U.K. Edition) - edited
1980 Evangelism Explosion Handbook
1980 Prison to Pulpit (Marshall Pickering)
1981 Hitch-Hiker's Guide to Heaven
1990 Prison to Pulpit (2nd Edition)
1994 Good, Morning Disciple

Booklets
1980 Just Grace
1989 Hope Now
1989 Grow Now
1990 Recycled

Hope Now International Ministries
PO BOX 325
Southampton
SO16 3AB
ENGLAND

PO BOX 4929
Dallas
Texas 75208
USA